UNSEEN STRENGTHS

Buruuj Tunsill

UNSEEN STRENGTHS

Navigating Intersectionality of Race and Disability in the Workplace

Black Studies

Collection Editor
Christopher Mcauley

LPp

First published in 2025 by Lived Places Publishing

British Library Cataloguing in Publication Data
A CIP record for this book is available from the British Library.

ISBN: 9781917566186 (pbk)
ISBN: 9781917566209 (ePDF)
ISBN: 9781917566193 (ePUB)

The right of Buruuj Tunsill to be identified as the Author of this work has been asserted by them in accordance with the Copyright, Design and Patents Act 1988.

Cover design by Fiachra McCarthy
Book design by Rachel Trolove of Twin Trail Design
Typeset by Newgen Publishing, UK

Lived Places Publishing
P.O. Box 1845
47 Echo Avenue
Miller Place, NY 11764

www.livedplacespublishing.com

Abstract

This memoir is the story of a Black woman living with schizoaffective disorder as she navigates identity, mental health, motherhood, and workplace adversity. Beginning with early symptoms and a formative manic episode, the narrative follows her experiences at Howard University and the resulting cultural disconnection. Subsequent chapters explore her transition into single motherhood, the pursuit of stability through work, and challenges within toxic professional environments shaped by racial and gendered hierarchies. Through a deeply personal lens, this memoir illustrates the impact of intersectionality on mental health, and the concluding chapter reflects on healing, growth, and strategies for sustaining wellness and identity.

Key words

Schizoaffective disorder, Black identity, Mental health, Intersectionality, Single motherhood, Cultural disconnection, Workplace trauma, Racial dynamics, K-12 Education System

Contents

Learning objectives

- Analyze the impact of mental health diagnoses on Black identity formation within the context of systemic racism, cultural expectations, and historical stigma in Black communities.
- Examine the intersections of race, gender, and mental health as they shape lived experiences of marginalization, resilience, and self-discovery.
- Critically engage with the challenges faced by Black women in professional and educational spaces, particularly within hierarchical and toxic workplace cultures.
- Explore the cultural disconnection and community response to mental illness through the lens of a Black woman navigating both personal and collective identity.
- Reflect on the role of single motherhood as a site of resistance, agency, and stability within the broader narrative of survival in Black life and culture.

Prelude

This chapter introduces the symptoms of schizoaffective disorder, recounts experiences before attending Howard University, details the first manic episode, and explores the lack of identity

As a child, I rarely spoke and often found myself isolated, retreating into an imaginary world. The world I created in my head was far better than reality—people were kinder, I had a loving husband, and a beautiful house. It was simply wonderful. As I grew older, my imaginary world evolved. It became my safe haven, a place where I didn't feel pain, wasn't hurt, and had complete control. If I had to pinpoint the root cause of my dissociative traits, I would say it was witnessing the abuse my mother endured and my father's absence. My family was dysfunctional and divided. After my dad left, the chaos continued, as my older siblings often fought. As time passed, the need for a functional family diminished because my alternate world felt more real to me.

I often found myself dissociating, but dissociation wasn't the only issue I struggled with. As a teenager, I developed hypochondria, which led me to spend hours lying in bed, consumed by paranoia. This constant anxiety eventually resulted in insomnia, which began in my junior year of high school and persisted into college. In the months leading up to my extended and involuntary hospitalization in a psychiatric institution, I became obsessed with illnesses and ailments. I rushed to the emergency room multiple times, convinced I was dying from HIV (human immunodeficiency virus) complications after having unprotected sex. I feared I had contracted the virus, and my mind spiraled, filled with endless scenarios of what could be wrong with me. In the end, I was simply suffering from acute bronchitis. But those irrational thoughts were just the tip of the iceberg. The insomnia, paired with my constant worry, led me to uncover a deeper set of issues that had been lurking beneath the surface.

Due to my constant detachment from reality and emotional dysregulation, my academic performance occasionally suffered. By high school, my behaviors began to manifest more outwardly. I found myself triggered more frequently, leading to belligerent outbursts and a few referrals. I remember one day when three teachers pulled me aside privately, recommending anger management. High school was filled with futile drama, friends, boys, and work. It was at work where I discovered my inability to control my temper. I started working at JCPenney at the age of sixteen, and while I appreciated the paycheck, being surrounded by so many people all day drained me. On top of that, I had to deal with co-workers who were often ill-equipped and, at times, hostile. I constantly questioned whether the effort was worth the outcome—a small paycheck for encountering a variety of personalities five days a week? By the end of high school, the combination of working a meaningless job and dealing with teenage drama sparked a strong desire to leave my hometown for good.

Unfortunately, I didn't get accepted into my dream school—Howard University. My failure to prepare was the reason for my failure. I couldn't focus on studying for the SAT (Scholastic

Assessment Test) and ACT (American College Testing), which resulted in scores that were less than satisfactory. Eager to leave my current home, I decided to enroll in a community college in Tallahassee to be closer to my sister. The transition from high school to college was liberating. During that time, I became more focused on my studies, adopted a more conservative mindset, and developed a newfound love for writing poetry. Living life without the distractions of sex, being surrounded by childhood friends, and enhancing my writing skills created a natural high unlike anything I'd ever experienced before. My creativity knew no bounds, and I'd wake up in the middle of the night just to write. However, my intense writing was just one sign of the overwhelming energy I felt, which soon led to a loss of control.

In March 2010, I can't recall the exact date, but I know that's when my life began to spiral out of control due to a deep disconnect between my mind, body, and soul. I felt as if I were possessed, as though something beyond myself was in control. Before my family knew it, I was gone—mentally absent. I was away for approximately three months, and I had to rely on my family's accounts to understand what I did during that time. My mother described me as being "dead" because I wasn't myself, one of my sisters compared me to the girl from *The Exorcist*, and my dad believed a demon had taken over me. Doctors diagnosed me with Schizoaffective disorder. Regardless of how anyone perceived it, I wasn't myself, and as a result of my absence, my sister had to withdraw me from school. My plan was to transfer to Howard after a year, but instead of moving closer to my goals, I found myself set back an entire year.

According to the National Alliance on Mental Illness (NAMI), schizoaffective disorder affects 0.3% of the population. Schizoaffective disorder, bipolar type, is characterized by episodes of mania and severe depression, accompanied by delusions and hallucinations. Specifically, individuals may experience the following symptoms:

- Disorganized thoughts (jumping from one topic to another without connecting ideas)
- Hallucinations (seeing or hearing things that are not there)
- Delusions (false beliefs)
- Manic behaviors (racing thoughts, euphoria, risky behaviors, aggression, feeling overly confident)
- Catatonic symptoms (being unable to move or appearing in a daze, stuck)
- Reduced range of emotions
- Lack of interest in activities
- Changes in sleep patterns
- Lack of motivation
- Suicidal thoughts
- Difficulty concentrating or remembering things
- Feelings of hopelessness or negativity

Additionally, symptoms may worsen due to stressful events, substance abuse (including drugs and alcohol), and some researchers suggest a genetic or brain chemistry component. Regardless of the cause, one thing is certain: adverse environmental factors, such as the place of work or frequently visited locations, can exacerbate symptoms.

Less than a year after the onset of symptoms, I continued my life as if it were just a rare occurrence that would not happen again. I shared my experiences with co-workers, and for the first time, I realized how ignorant people can be. At the tender age of nineteen, I was in school and working at JCPenney to make a living. I worked in a hectic, hostile work environment where "the customer is always right" and associates were just gossipy individuals who lacked adventure in their lives. I recall sharing my story with an older Hispanic woman from New York, and before I knew it, she was running around telling others my story and warning them to be careful around me because I could snap at any moment. Another older Asian woman, who was my supervisor at the time, pulled me aside and told me to keep my business to myself because people talk. The moment I realized I was being viewed as a threat to some based on a diagnosis was the moment I began to attempt to dissociate from the occurrence completely. Being a woman, which I had always deemed inferior based on my upbringing; being Black, which society deems a threat; being Muslim, which society views as a terrorist; and now dealing with a mental illness that carries stigma? I never really spent much time situating myself in society. I just lived life, doing what I was "supposed" to do and pursuing my goals. However, something felt off. I felt different, alone, and no longer understood who I was or who I really wanted to be.

1
Who am I? The struggle of diagnosis and disconnection from Black modern culture

This chapter reflects on my two years at Howard University, high-lighting both the positive aspects and challenges within the Black community. It discusses feelings of rejection following a manic episode, which further disconnected me from my cultural identity.

Culture can be defined in many ways. Often, when people think of culture, they associate it with language, nationality, or race/ethnicity. While these are certainly aspects of culture, there are other elements that are frequently overlooked, such as individual disability/ability, social class, and gender. There are three types of culture: overt, covert, and subtle. Overt culture refers to the obvious differences, such as language or the way someone dresses. Covert culture, however, is implicit and often goes unrecognized by its members unless they engage in self-reflection. Last, subtle culture involves recognizing the underlying values and beliefs that influence one's actions. Culture is not a fixed concept; it is continually redefined by each individual's unique experiences. It shapes the worldview of most people. For me, however, due to my tendency to retreat into my imaginary world, I never gave much thought to how I viewed myself or the world around me. As a result, I wasn't fully aware of my covert and subtle culture. When it comes to my overt culture, yes, I was raised Muslim, identify as Black, and am recognized as a woman, but I can't say I fully connect with any of these identities. After spending a year catching up on college credits at a local community college in South Florida, I finally arrived at Howard University in the fall of 2011. Being a college student on an HBCU (Historically Black College or University) campus was a new experience that pushed me to examine myself and the world around me.

The desire to attend Howard University stemmed from advice my older sister gave me: to choose a college that best aligned with my goals. After some research, I found that Howard University was an excellent school for those pursuing a career in journalism. It also helped that I learned my favorite actress, Taraji P. Henson, and my favorite video jockey, LaLa Vazquez, had both attended this school. Beyond that, the prospect of being surrounded by other Black students with similar aspirations was inspiring, and perhaps most importantly, it offered me a chance to get away from Florida. I envisioned Howard as a place where I would be surrounded by individuals with a strong sense of community and greater knowledge. However, my expectations quickly proved to be inaccurate.

On my first night in the dorm, I met two young women who became my acquaintances: one from the Virgin Islands and the other from New York. Both appeared humble and friendly. One was religious and involved with the campus choir, while the other seemed more like a free spirit and was also in the School of Communication, like me. My first night was positive, and I was excited about attending my classes.

During my first week, I received a syllabus and assignments that were due sooner than expected. I was especially excited about the Intro to Mass Communication class because I'd get the chance to test out my journalism skills. However, the class was taught by an older White woman who didn't quite resonate with me. Her rigid rules made it feel like we were children, and her approach failed to capture my attention. Initially, I was uncertain about her as a professor, but that quickly changed after I received my grade on my first paper. I had written about FOX News and its blatant racism, supporting my arguments with credible sources, but I received a C. Since I was used to getting A's, this grade was both frustrating and unacceptable. I requested to meet with her during office hours to discuss it. After a heated conversation on my part, she eventually changed my grade from a C to a B. The fact that it didn't take much convincing to get the grade adjusted made it clear that her grading was subjective, and she had taken my stance on FOX News too personally. As a result, I decided the best choice for me was to withdraw from the class and reconsider my future career plans. Her attitude was very off-putting, and my passion for journalism diminished. So I switched my major from journalism to Communication and Culture, with a focus on legal communication. I figured the writing I would be doing in this field would be more concrete, leaving little room for subjective grading.

Immersing myself in the remainder of my classes was exciting, and I thoroughly enjoyed my professors' discussions. However, the students around me were not what I had envisioned. Many seemed to come from the bourgeoisie class, exuding a materialistic attitude and lacking an understanding of community. I'm not one to force friendships, so I continued to navigate the campus on my own. As I walked up and down the hill to various classes, one thing that stood out to me was the campus' strong affiliation with sororities and fraternities. I was familiar with popular organizations like AKA (Alpha Kappa Alpha) and DST (Delta Sigma Theta), but I decided that my education was more important than joining a group of what I perceived as snobbish individuals who had forgotten where they came from. I could often spot their affiliations by their pearls and sweaters, but to me, it seemed as though many joined for a sense of security or belonging rather than for the values of community, scholarship, leadership, and service. While everyone seemed preoccupied with fitting in, I stayed focused on my grades and on meeting my graduation goal—2013.

However, my new desire to stay mostly to myself didn't quite pan out. Due to wearing a hijab or head covering, I was often approached by other Muslims on campus. One guy invited me to join the Muslim Student Association (MSA), and since I wasn't particularly drawn to the overall culture of the school, I figured that being among other Muslims wouldn't hurt—it would likely be the closest I'd come to finding a sense of community. The guy invited me to walk downtown DC (District of Columbia) with other Muslim students, and my new acquaintance from the Virgin Islands joined me. The exploration was fun, and I developed a little crush on the guy who had invited me. I also cultivated relationships with two other Caribbean American Muslim girls, "T" and "B," with whom I would soon spend quite a bit of time.

I learned at a young age that my personality isn't for everyone, which is why I tended to keep to myself. I often blurted out things that might offend others or failed to display the kind of decorum that most people preferred. Yet, for some reason, people always seemed to gravitate toward me. As time went on, more people approached me for various reasons, each with different intentions. I can openly admit that I tended to be open with anyone who approached me because I simply didn't see the harm in expressing myself or revealing my true thoughts on any subject. While most didn't take a liking to it, I did develop some friendships with people who appreciated my personality.

In some of my classes, I had to complete group projects. In one class, Computers and Society, I ended up in a group with a student named "D," who had a southern drawl from North Carolina. Initially, I didn't care to be in the same group as him because he had once complimented me on my shoes, and for some reason, I didn't like when people complimented me. It made me feel awkward and uncomfortable, as if I were suddenly on display for judgment. But to my surprise, D turned out to be a laid-back, chill guy. We ended up having other classes together, where we started sitting together, developed inside jokes, and built a mutual respect for each other.

D also showed me the respect I deserved. Every time we walked on the sidewalk, he would pull me by the arm to the inside, saying, "Now, B, you know I don't play like that. Girls are not supposed to walk close to the road." I had never known that was proper decorum, and he taught me something new. In another instance, he demonstrated his respect when I felt his girlfriend was rude for interrupting our conversation without saying "excuse me." A few days later, he walked over to me with her in the iLab and insisted that she apologize. She hadn't even realized what she had done. While he was just my friend, he showed me how I would want to be treated in an intimate relationship.

Aside from my new cultivated relationship with D, I became involved in MSA and also spent quite a bit of my time in the School of Communication. During off-campus hours, I spent a lot of time with the two Muslim girls, working in the admissions office, or working at JCPenney. Most of my fall semester was spent talking about my crush, who seemed completely oblivious to the fact that I liked him. Since he wasn't giving me any attention, I spent my days gossiping and talking negatively about him to my friends out of bitterness.

As I networked around the school, I noticed pockets of humble people who kept to themselves. Some were focused on sorority and fraternity life, others were more spiritually inclined, and some were deeply dedicated to their religion, whether Islam or Christianity. Then there were those who barely showed up. It was clear that there was a dominant macroculture of students who knew how to navigate the school and finesse their way through. I can honestly say that the majority of students knew how to talk a good game to earn their place within the school; however, the hard work I expected to see from many of them was often missing.

Concurrently, working at a major mall in the DMV (District of Columbia, Maryland, and Virginia) area exposed me to more people from DC, offering a broader view of the world beyond college. This experience gave me a deeper understanding of how the world worked, and it created a disconcerting feeling within me. Ultimately, it fostered a growing distrust of the world around me. There was one instance with a young Black female co-worker who often tried to get free meals from others, including me. She would tell a sob story about being abused and forced to abort multiple babies by her abusive partner. She was definitely a likable person, but I quickly began to notice that she often tried to throw herself a pity party to get a free lunch. On the one hand, it's like "get it how you live," and on the other, it revealed to me that many people lack authenticity and genuineness.

The organizations I was associating with—from the university to JCPenney—felt misaligned with my morals and ethics. I found myself asking: Had I sheltered myself too much? Why was it so easy for people to skate by without truly earning their place? Is this how most people act? Numerous questions swirled in my mind, but once again, I had to remain focused on the reason I was there. My relationships with work-study co-workers, classmates, and professors continued to evolve. Despite the disconnect with the masses, it wasn't difficult to focus on cultivating authentic connections. At the end of the day, I knew we were all there to complete a degree or move on to something bigger and better, but human connections and interactions are an essential part of life—whether we admit it or not.

As I continued to develop new connections, the fall semester began to move a little faster. After homecoming, Thanksgiving quickly rolled around. I spent my time with "T" and "B" and video chatting with my family since I couldn't afford to travel for such a short period. These girls welcomed me into their home and really made me feel comfortable. Oftentimes, we had raw conversations about various things, but I often found myself talking about the Muslim guy who didn't want me. I thought I had found a safe space with "T" and "B" to say whatever I felt, as they would listen and offer their feedback or thoughts.

As time passed, I found someone new to crush on; eventually, my thoughts about the Muslim guy faded. By the time the spring semester rolled around, I was transitioning into new classes, new crushes, and meeting new people. During that semester, I started speaking up more in class, leading discussions, and adjusting to life as a Howard student. I spent a lot of time in the iLab, where students typically go to study, and it was there that I met a consistent Muslim friend named Muammon. He was of Middle Eastern descent from Maryland and majored in engineering. He showed a genuine interest in being a friend—offering me food, rides, and any kind of help I needed, which was pretty rare on campus.

Aside from my friend "D," Muammon was another person I fully trusted. Around the same time, I met more pleasant Muslim women; the Muslim community on campus was tight-knit. They were often the ones who showed the most interest in helping me out, whether by offering assistance or simply hanging out with me.

In one of my most boring classes, I also managed to form an alliance with some classmates to get through the semester. One thing I noticed about Howard students is that they communicate with purpose—they get to know you if you can serve a purpose for them. I can't say many genuine connections were made, but if your goals aligned with theirs, you could build some meaningful academic relationships.

Unfortunately for me, I tend to genuinely care about people when I meet them and I always want to help however I can. It's just the way I am. Nevertheless, the consequence of constantly meeting new people is the harsh realization that others often cannot and will not show up for you the way you show up for them. Once the need for you is over, so is the "camaraderie." This is a lesson I had to repeatedly learn through my experiences in work and school.

To be honest, I understood the dynamic of the Black individual: at the end of the day, we often have to work twice as hard to prove ourselves or find ways to finesse the system in order to earn our spot in society. The mentality of individuals on campus, especially within my specific school, was understandable but disheartening, as I was someone who deeply desired authentic connections.

That being said, not all of the relationships I formed were negative. Through one connection, I landed a full scholarship for my senior year. While some relationships were growing, others were slowly fading. One thing I've learned about myself is that I'm generally tolerable on a surface level, but once I become comfortable with someone, my bluntness can become a problem. For example, one of the first girls I connected with became increasingly frustrated with me because she felt I was judgmental. I had called a tattoo she wanted to get "ghetto," which upset her.

As the spring semester came to an end, the two sisters, "T" and "B," ended our "friendship" because they were upset about how I had talked about my crush. Although the conversations about him had only lasted for about four months, they chose to express their dismay months later, via text. I've never understood why some people hold their thoughts and feelings in for so long, only to explode later. If they had truly considered me a friend, I thought an open and honest conversation would have been more appropriate. Sadly, the end of that friendship left me in tears, but it also forced me to reflect on my behavior and make improvements.

As some may say, c'est la vie (such is life). The spring semester ended on a bittersweet note. I successfully completed all my courses, landed a scholarship, and gained a deeper understanding of the school's culture, but I also lost connections that I thought were genuine.

Throughout that summer, I stayed in touch with Muammon, D, and, of course, my high school classmate who also attended Howard. I started to develop hidden feelings for Muammon, but I knew that a relationship between us would never work due to our cultural differences. Still, I decided to hold on to our friendship until it inevitably came to an end, likely due to his eventual marriage. The reality that many of my friendships would eventually fade, one way or another, became a sad truth I had to accept.

One spiritual and insightful young lady once told me, "Just because we separate or I am not here doesn't mean I am not still here for you." I held on to those words, and from that moment forward, I made an effort not to become too attached to people. Instead, I began to appreciate that everyone who enters your life serves a purpose, and while their presence is meaningful, I had to learn not to shatter when they inevitably leave.

Entering the fall semester, I knew I had to maintain a tunnel vision. I was taking nine classes—more than the recommended course load—and because of my solid GPA, I was approved to take the maximum number of credits. Fall 2012 revealed the hierarchy within the School of Communication, showing how those involved in certain honor societies received privileges others didn't. The laziness among the student population became more apparent. My frustration and anger grew as I led group projects time after time due to my distrust of others. Some students seemed entitled and didn't prioritize their major classes. At this point, I had been pegged as the responsible one. In most of my major courses, I felt exploited.

On multiple occasions, I did all the work for group assignments. In one group, I completed everyone's portion, and all they had to do was present. Despite my hard work, I received a lower grade than the guy who presented the work I had done—simply because he was part of the honor society. In another group, a student demanded to present on a section she hadn't contributed to. I thought I was giving her an easy task, but she ended up taking credit for it. I was always the one to lead, but I wanted everyone to be satisfied even if they didn't put in the effort. It was in these moments that I truly understood the importance of speaking well and affiliating with the right people. I also began to notice a trend among the most successful students at Howard—they were all exceptional speakers. While they were great at grasping topics and acing exams, I found myself carrying more of the weight in group projects. Their priorities seemed to be more focused on the hustle and their social lives, including crossing over into fraternities or sororities.

During the fall semester, more people started to associate with me because of my strong work ethic. I became the person others turned to when they needed help. At that time, I didn't mind, as I simply wanted everyone to succeed. However, I had my boundaries, which were questioned by one of my professors during class. It was the beginning of my last semester, and I had rented my textbook, fully prepared for class. In a room with approximately twenty to twenty-five students, I was the only one who had made the effort to obtain the book. Many students found other ways to get through the class, but this time, it seemed we actually needed the book.

The professor pointed out that we were a "family," and that family helps each other. She then requested that I pass my book around so others could make copies. My jaw dropped. I couldn't bring myself to say that I didn't feel like the majority of these people were my family. Perhaps she held that "family" mentality because she was older and from a different generation, but she didn't know those students. In fact, half of them hadn't even spoken to me. I'm usually quiet and keep to myself to avoid confrontation or being disliked. I don't need everyone to like me, but I certainly don't want to be someone others dislike.

But this time, I had to speak up. Despite my usual avoidance of conflict, I didn't feel comfortable just passing my book along. I asked publicly, "How can I trust that I'll get my book back when these students weren't responsible enough to prepare for class?" The professor made an example of me, framing it as if I didn't value family, which felt like an attempt to guilt me into complying. And unfortunately, it worked. I ended up passing my book along, but only under the condition that I monitor who makes copies.

The more encounters I had with people, the more I learned about societal structures. I consistently found myself having to be mindful of what I said, as my words often ruffled a few feathers. D, Muammon, and a couple of others at my work-study job were the only ones I felt completely comfortable being myself around. I don't like upsetting people, but I was never taught to hold my tongue just to avoid offending others. At the time, the "lost friendships" didn't impact me because, in reality, having one solid, authentic friend is enough. On top of that, I met random people who provided me with delightful conversations or helpful assistance.

At the beginning of my time at Howard, I was closely involved with the MSA, but as time went on, I began to notice a disconnect within the group. Many people didn't like the MSA president, judging him for his confidence in who he was and in his ability to lead. Once again, I felt uncomfortable because of the inauthentic attitudes of others, so I started associating with Muslim students individually rather than as a group. Most of my time, however, was spent with D, as we shared the same classes and therefore similar schedules. Every day, we would meet by the twin dorms to walk to class, and on some days, we would have lunch at Potbelly.

Days spent with D were never boring. When an arrogant student would speak rudely toward a professor or act too self-assured, D and I would exchange looks, as if to say, "Who does this girl think she is?" Then D would make a clever joke that would often humble her, if she happened to overhear. When we had time to ourselves, D and I would discuss religion, politics, and our personal goals. The light that surrounded D's aura made me forget the overall culture at the school; he was the embodiment of the Howard I had envisioned.

While D was my closest friend at Howard, every so often, I would spend time with my high school friend at her off-campus dorm. She knew me better than most, so I felt more comfortable around her, but she also wore a facade, like many other Howard students. I completely understand that people evolve as they get older, but it seemed some were more focused on maintaining a certain appearance. My friend, along with her roommate, exhibited this in many ways. As a result, I often had to bite my tongue to avoid outwardly judging them. Truthfully, I was better off spending time alone, as I could trust my own company.

As my workload increased, I became more focused on maintaining my grades. As the fall semester grew more hectic, I found myself spending less time with D. We would meet up in iLab to study, and during that time, I noticed he seemed a little sluggish. During homecoming, he fell and hit his head. In the days leading up to the fall, he had been complaining of a headache and mentioned that the sun bothered his eyes. While I was concerned, I didn't want my hypochondria to influence his actions, so I kept my worries to myself.

When the fall semester came to an end, D and I said our goodbyes, unaware that it would be the last time I would see him. On December 20, 2012, during my winter break, I received a text from my friend while I was working. She asked me what I was doing and said she would wait until I got off; but my anxiety was overwhelming, so I called her to ask what was going on. She told me that one of our classmates had passed away. I guessed one student I was close with, but she said, "No, it's someone closer to you." I didn't want to ask, but I just knew it couldn't have been D. I hesitantly said, "Not D?" She replied, "Yes."

My heart dropped into my stomach. Standing in the dressing room, I quickly composed myself enough to ask the manager if I could take a break. I hung up the phone, and as soon as I stepped outside, tears started pouring from my eyes. D had dreams. He was a preacher with plans to pursue his PhD. He was young, a true gentleman, and authentic. While we didn't share the same faith, we understood each other, and he respected and accepted me. He was the closest person to me at Howard. I was just in disbelief. The one true friend I had met outside of Florida was gone, and I had no choice but to accept it. My grandmother had passed away when I was younger, but we weren't close. D was a friend, and his loss marked the first time I had experienced the death of someone truly close to me. The toll it took on me was immense.

In my last semester, the spring semester, I had eight classes on my caseload, and I had to somehow maintain tunnel vision.

When we returned that semester, a service was held for D, but I did not attend. Mourning with others was not something I felt ready to participate in. I stayed in my dorm during that time, in silence and in a complete daze. I tried to act as if D wasn't gone, as if he had just gone off on a trip somewhere. I found myself dissociating, something I hadn't done in a while.

Lying in bed, I feel a warm rush of air across my body. I close my eyes and hear D's voice, reassuring me that he is okay. A smile spreads across my face as I communicate with him, remaining in bed. I go through my days, focused in the classroom, but always returning to my dorm to spend time with D. I don't realize that what I'm experiencing are hallucinations—the voice feels so real to me—that I continue on as if everything is normal.

However, within a few weeks, things take a sharp turn. My adrenaline surges, and I feel an overwhelming sense of euphoria. I'm ecstatic—my friend hasn't truly left; he's just physically gone, but he's still here. I begin talking to various adults in the School of Communication, sharing the insights I've received, without worrying about how I might appear. As my thoughts grow more intense, the changes are most evident in my dialectic conversations in class, and my writing reflects these shifts as well. In my Intra-Interpersonal Communication class, I'm required to explore who I am psychologically, spiritually, emotionally, and physically. It's at this moment that I realize I don't connect with being a woman or the causes women fight for. I don't identify with many of the Black students at Howard, and I begin to question my religion. I don't even relate to the diagnosis I was given.

I start to understand that a large part of my identity is tied to being spiritually sensitive—I feel spirits, both of the living and the dead. It feels as though I'm receiving messages from a higher spiritual source. What I'm discovering about myself feels completely different from the culture around me. People see me as strange, but to me, it's a profound part of who I am.

As time passes, the voices in my head grow stronger. I reach out to one of my professors for help, and while she tries to communicate with my other professors, I struggle to navigate DC and take care of myself. One day, I get lost on the train and can't find my way back home. My friend from high school reached out to help. She brought me to her off-campus dorm, even though I insisted on staying in my dorm. After a few hours of listening to my rants, she became frightened, as did her friend. Without warning, police officers entered the room while my friend was allegedly at the store.

I don't trust the police, especially when I'm unstable. They told me I had to leave, and I had no idea where to go or where my friend was. As I'm escorted downstairs, still ranting, I overheard a Black security guard speaking negatively about me, as if I've done something wrong. I became belligerent and started arguing with her. In the middle of the altercation, one of my classmates saw me. She saw me like no one ever has before—she knew what I was going through and she understood that it was much more than a mental episode. She calmed the security guard down and asked if she could use an empty room to talk to me. My classmate's boyfriend wrote down everything I said in the quiet room. Later that night, my classmate drove me back to my dorm, but my friend was nowhere to be found.

Eventually, I found myself in a psychiatric ward in DC for a few days. When I returned, my classmate enlightened me on my friend's behavior. She told me that my friend had planned to put me on the train. At that moment, I was devastated. How could someone who's known me for over six years neglect me like that, while someone who barely knew me would go out of their way to help? My classmate didn't speak negatively about my friend but advised me to be cautious, suggesting that not everyone has my best interests at heart. She explained that my friend's other friend was influencing her and that her friend's mom was telling her to distance herself from me.

I don't remember threatening anyone; I simply tried to explain what was happening to me and how it might evolve. If anyone was scared, it was me, because I knew the uncertain future that someone like me faced. During my crisis, there were a few people who did their best to protect and defend me. While many saw me as crazy, others listened and told me my thoughts made sense. However, it was that one classmate who truly made me feel heard. She told me I had a gift and connected me to someone who could help me understand it. I now realize I was receiving spiritual messages, but I didn't know how to process them or keep them to myself, and the world around me only labeled me as crazy.

The urge to share my insights without coming across as delusional was incredibly difficult for me. I spent the majority of my time talking to the person my classmate recommended, who helped me better understand myself. Still, my mind continued to race at high speed. After being released from the hospital, I tried to maintain some sense of stability. However, my behavior seemed unusual to those around me, and my ability to refrain from rambling became impossible.

I remember one conversation with a professor who had once told me that I would make an excellent researcher. We were sitting in her office discussing my future plans when I distinctly recall telling her that I was no longer going to graduate school because I was "crazy" and that it wasn't meant for people like me. She looked at me seriously and told me not to say that ever again. The weight of being Black with a mental health diagnosis hit me hard—it felt like an ongoing battle. I think my professor didn't want me to voice something so negative, especially as a Black individual like myself.

My internal struggles were becoming more intense. One day, in a pre-law class, I suddenly blurted out profanity. My professor, who was also an attorney, looked shocked. While I can't recall exactly what she said, I remember her pointing toward the door. I left the class, and no one followed to check on me. That was the last time I heard from her. Not once did she reach out to see how I was doing. In hindsight, I still don't understand why she chose to dismiss me without questioning my behavior, especially when it was clearly out of the norm.

Luckily, a few classmates who witnessed my behavior stepped up to help me without asking for anything in return. They didn't really know me, but they could tell I needed someone to protect me from the outside world. Unfortunately, most people don't carry that level of empathy. From others, I was simply judged and written off, which later made me realize this is common in the Black community. Generally, Black people support you in minor matters, but once you deviate from the social norm, you become an outcast. It doesn't matter how many people once relied on you or how many you've inspired. Once you appear unfit, the number of people willing to help you dwindles, and you feel like you're deemed futile by the community.

My experience at Howard forced me to grow mentally, emotionally, and spiritually. I met some incredible people there, but more importantly, I encountered individuals who made me confront myself. I also came to realize how ignorant and insensitive some people can be, which taught me that I needed to learn to function as my true self, without relying on others. The Black modern culture I observed was centered on image, maintaining a facade, and avoiding vulnerability. In that world, being vulnerable meant weakness, and weakness could prevent you from meeting the high expectations you set for yourself. Ultimately, it was a culture I couldn't conform to, even if I had the ability or desire to do so. I found myself surrounded by an ego-driven culture, all this while I was being pushed to meet my higher self. I discovered new parts of who I was by disconnecting from the larger culture I had immersed myself in for two years. Those two years passed quickly, and I was left unsure of what came next. Could I even be a part of this world without being rejected?

2
Decision in motherhood: Choosing stability through work

This chapter examines my journey into single motherhood, focusing on the tough decision to seek stable employment while raising two children.

On June 18, 2014, I gave birth to my son, a life-changing event. After graduating from Howard University and after being released from the hospital, I was still not completely stable. Shortly after graduation, I made an impulsive decision to move to Virginia with a man I barely knew. He was much older than me, forced me to do things I didn't want to do, and was verbally and physically abusive. After about four months of living with him, I left because he slapped me. My family encouraged me to come home; so after spending a month in a hotel, my sister came to pick me up and drove me and my car back to Florida.

When someone experiences a manic episode and then comes down from it, it takes time to return to a "normal" state of mind. Unfortunately, my family didn't understand that I was making an impulsive decision. I was old enough to make my own choices, but part of me wishes they had stopped me. Despite the turmoil with a man I barely knew, I was blessed with the birth of a wonderful boy; however, the arrival of my son forced me to think about how I would provide for him and keep a roof over his head.

Because I had been hospitalized for consecutive months, I was eligible for total permanent disability, but it came with restrictions. I couldn't earn more than USD 16,000 a year for three consecutive years. Given these limitations, I became a substitute teacher and worked as a mobile sales associate at Best Buy. Still, these weren't enough to support my child. I had to hustle under the table to make ends meet, which included babysitting, doing hair, and any other work I could find that paid. I couldn't afford childcare, so I offered food stamps and whatever I could to have my sister watch my son until we had a falling out. That's when someone who's like a second son to me stepped in to babysit my son, without pay. Most days, I worked from early in the morning until late at night, and the only thing I could do when I got home was nurse my son to sleep.

I knew that after three years, I would be free, and my son and I could move out of Florida—maybe to DC or Atlanta, where I could focus on writing my book. I wanted to be a writer, but I knew I had to focus on substantial responsibilities at that moment so my son could have a stable life. Neither of my jobs were stressful. As a substitute teacher, I had the freedom to work when I wanted, which was perfect since I had to limit my income, and there were days when I didn't want to work. I visited different schools and didn't have to adapt to any harmful organizational culture. Some schools felt like a prison, while others were vibrant, but most of the schools I visited had students with behavioral problems. I didn't spend too much time getting to know the staff members; I just went in and did my job.

My job at Best Buy was pretty chill—the rules weren't too rigid. I went in, provided satisfactory customer service, and activated phones. My manager was a young guy who gave guidance when needed but didn't micromanage. At Best Buy, I worked in a market-driven culture where both managers and associates focused on profit margins and company growth.

After frequently working at one particular elementary school, I was hired as a paraprofessional, which gave me some stability while still working part-time at Best Buy. As a paraprofessional, I had set hours but didn't carry the same responsibilities as a teacher, nor did I deal with the same level of stress. I was familiar with the school and many of the teachers since it was my former elementary school. The school had a clan organizational culture—family-like, with people working together to improve students' reading skills and test scores. However, for educators, there were issues with the current administrator. According to some teachers, the principal had no compassion and had a business mindset, trying to get rid of a lot of teachers. In fact, the principal was successful in getting rid of several teachers, but I made sure to stay out of those conversations because I didn't want anything disturbing my peace. More importantly, their issues didn't really concern me.

There was one instance when I saw a fairly new teacher crying over something the principal had said. Another time, the principal and assistant principal (AP) were discussing something, and the principal turned to me and asked if I wanted to become a teacher. I laughed and confidently replied, "No, I'm not going to be here long. I'm a writer."

The idea of being tied down to any job didn't sit well with me. I needed freedom. I didn't want the obligation of teaching kids because once I signed a contract to teach children for a school year, I knew I'd have to follow through, even if I didn't want to, and I couldn't be a teacher who walked out on kids mid-year. Additionally, if a principal thought they could make me cry, I was sure to lose my job because I didn't tolerate disrespect or anyone talking down to me. I still had trouble controlling my temper when it came to dictatorial bosses who lacked the ability to lead. My goal was to remain in a peaceful state of mind while I rode out those three years.

Additionally, during my time as a paraprofessional, I built meaningful relationships with both my co-workers and the students I worked with daily. The school's culture provided a supportive environment where I could focus on my responsibilities without unnecessary stress. Each day, I walked into work with a joyous smile, feeling at ease in my role. What made the experience even more special was working closely with a teacher who had once been my second grade educator. The familiarity of that relationship made the job even more comfortable, allowing me to thrive in my position.

This positive energy carried over into my second job at Best Buy, where the laid-back atmosphere made it easier to balance my responsibilities despite the sales quotas. Even with the pressure of meeting goals, I never felt overwhelmed.

However, while my professional life was running smoothly, my personal life was becoming increasingly strained, particularly in my relationship with my sister. She was my primary babysitter, and my long work hours were taking a toll on her. Some nights, I also took on a side hustle as a babysitter, which meant I couldn't arrive to pick up my son until around midnight. The strain on our relationship grew, and the tension between us became palpable. My inability to consistently adhere to our agreed-upon schedule triggered arguments and left me feeling anxious. Despite my sister's frustrations, I knew I had to continue working multiple jobs to provide for my child and maintain financial stability.

As time passed at the school, I developed close connections with some of my male co-workers, one of whom I found myself particularly drawn to. What initially started as an innocent crush quickly escalated into a complicated and messy situation. His ex, the mother of his child, started working at the school after we had already become involved. The culture of the workplace remained familiar, but I began to feel a shift—an undercurrent of jealousy and unspoken tension. It was as if she knew about my involvement with him, though she never explicitly addressed it. She would speak to me casually when he wasn't around, but the moment he entered the room, she ignored me completely. Despite this, I remained cordial, as I had no reason to harbor any ill feelings toward her. However, I chose to keep my personal life discreet, focusing on maintaining my peace while juggling my responsibilities.

Our fleeting involvement lasted only four to five months before my reckless decisions caught up with me—I discovered I was pregnant in January 2016. At that moment, my world felt as if it had come to a screeching halt. I didn't know what to do or who to turn to, but one thing became clear: I no longer wanted to work at the school. Not only was I unprepared for another child, but I also dreaded the inevitable judgment that would follow. Gossip spread quickly in that environment, and with my child's father being well known in the area, the scrutiny would have been unbearable. His ex, who many assumed was still his girl-friend, worked at the school, which only added to my distress.

A few co-workers whom I had once considered friends sug-gested that I terminate the pregnancy. One even pointed out my living situation, questioning how I would manage with a one bedroom apartment. I didn't have answers to their questions, but I knew one thing for certain—aborting my child would have deeply affected my mental health. The baby's father had left the school for a new job before I found out about the pregnancy. When I shared the news with him, his reaction was cruel and dismissive—he accused me of ruining his life. I made it clear that his involvement was his choice, but I was moving forward regardless. Meanwhile, his ex continued to draw closer to me, as if she sensed something but was waiting for me to confirm it.

After much contemplation, I made the difficult decision to resign from my position as a paraprofessional and return to working as a substitute teacher. My abrupt departure raised suspicions, and it wasn't long before people noticed the shift in my demea-nor. I could no longer maintain the vibrant smile I once wore; the weight of my reality had taken its toll. My family scolded me for my reckless decisions, and the pressure of my circumstances became overwhelming. I needed a plan, a way to secure finan-cial stability.

The silver lining was that I had completed two out of the three years of my mandatory limited income due to being permanently disabled. By the end of 2016, I would be able to work full-time, but the uncertainty of where to go next loomed over me. I had envisioned a different path—one where I could finally escape once my older son turned four and no longer required daycare. However, my plans had unraveled, and my dream of becoming an author felt further out of reach.

As I worked as a substitute teacher at various schools, I spent much of my time contemplating my next move. Eventually, I realized that the most logical path forward was to pursue teaching certification. The irony of it all was that I had once laughed when my principal asked if I ever considered becoming a teacher; yet here I was, making the conscious decision to enter the profession. With this new goal in mind, I resigned from Best Buy and transitioned into working as a nanny. I finished the school year subbing at various schools, where I felt less pressured by workplace dynamics since I wasn't a permanent fixture in any of them.

Despite taking steps toward stability, I found myself working less and falling into periods of depression. My life was changing rapidly, and I wasn't sure if I was ready for what lay ahead. But ready or not, I had to prepare myself—because in just a few months, I would be welcoming another baby boy into the world. The road ahead was uncertain, but I was determined to navigate it the best way I could.

As summer ensued, I was on a mission to work yet another job to help make ends meet. At just shy of six months pregnant, I attempted to hide my pregnancy so I could land a job as a respite caregiver. The child I would be working with had a tendency to become aggressive, but primarily toward himself. I did not want to risk not being hired due to my pregnancy. With this position, I worked with a child with autism in his home while his mother navigated the household as needed. Since the job was just at home with the mother and two children—as the boy had a little sister—I did not have to experience any organizational culture per se. It felt family-like, and the family was very warm and welcoming. At times, the mother became increasingly frustrated due to the severity of her child's disability and needed space, but I never took it personally. The father always remained pleasant despite his wife's frustrations, and the warm environment allowed me to show up with a smile on my face, even though I was not the happiest version of myself.

While working multiple nanny jobs and serving as a respite caregiver, I was also preparing for my certification exam to become an educator. To get my foot in the door, I had to pass a four-part exam encompassing math, reading/language arts, science, and social studies in order to be certified to teach elementary education (K-6). I could start working full-time as a teacher in December 2016, but in the meantime, I needed to find a steady position from August to November to maintain a stable income. As summer progressed, I remained in a mellow mood. Some people found out I was pregnant, and rumors circulated about who the father could be. A guy I associated with at the school figured it out, but I neither confirmed nor denied his suspicions. Shortly after, the rumor mill at school picked up, and negative comments were made. However, I could not be bothered with the hearsay as I had far bigger concerns—I was about to have two children in an apartment meant for only two people. I planned to remain under the radar until I could afford something bigger, but I was unsure if that plan would work.

The father of my child had chosen to be absent shortly after I found out I was pregnant; however, toward the end of the summer, he reached out and asked if we could talk. He apologized for his previous actions and promised to remain active in his child's life. I had spent the majority of my pregnancy alone, just as I had with my first pregnancy, which placed me in a depressive mood. So, when my second son's father reached out, I was somewhat hopeful. Nonetheless, I knew I needed to ensure that my future was secure, so I remained focused on my goal of becoming an educator.

The first time I took the certification exam, I passed the ELA (English Language Arts)/Reading section and had to wait 30 days before retaking the other sections. The second time, I passed social studies and math but failed science once again. With my second son due in September, I knew I had only one more chance before I would have to reconsider my career path. I studied as much as possible for science, but by the end of August, I felt depleted. During the testing session, I sat in my seat, talked to myself, and reminded myself that this was my last opportunity before giving birth. I told myself not to overthink and to do the best I could. When I walked out of that testing session, the proctor smiled and said, "Congratulations." It was the first time I cried during my pregnancy—tears of joy, because I could now apply for jobs. That day marked the beginning of a hopeful journey with my two children. I walked out of that exam room with so much joy in my heart and a sense of relief. I had passed my exam and secured a job as a teaching assistant at a technical center high school. The environment was laid-back and the students were well behaved and ambitious, meaning that I would not have to deal with excessive stress.

My journey had not been easy, but in that moment, I felt a renewed sense of hope for the future.

As I settled into my role, I began to reflect not only on my personal growth but also on the culture of the school itself. Workplace environments can vary greatly, and I soon realized that my school operated differently from the traditional "family-like" atmosphere often found in education. Within the education field, many co-workers refer to each other as family, reflecting a clan culture; however, the school where I worked embodied more of an adhocracy culture. This type of culture focuses on innovation and growth, fostering psychological safety where workers feel secure in their positions. Additionally, it encourages an entrepreneurial approach, allowing employees to take risks and pursue new ideas. This environment suited me well, as I was a teacher assistant and did not feel pressured to take on extensive responsibilities.

At this technological school, I sat in the classroom while the teacher facilitated lessons online, with students working on computers. My role primarily involved monitoring student behavior and maintaining the classroom atmosphere as the teacher conducted lessons virtually. A few times a week, she would come to class in person, though sometimes she did not attend at all. Given that the students were mature sixteen-year olds, I rarely had to discipline them; I lacked the energy to be concerned with minor issues. I made it clear to them that they were in charge of their education and that I was not paid enough to be overly strict. They respected my laid-back approach.

During this time, I focused on writing and handling other personal matters as I was nearing my due date. The school schedule was early, which made my days feel short. Administrators did not bother me, and I rarely saw other staff members except when I visited the cafeteria for lunch. My days were quiet and peaceful—something I needed more than ever. Yet, more mental chaos was just around the corner.

One day, I visited my mother's school because she asked me to bring her food. While there, I was approached by the mother of the child of the man I had been involved with. She had the audacity to inquire about the father of my unborn child, attempting to make friendly conversation. However, I sensed an ulterior motive. In response to her question, I simply said, "No one." The truth was, the father of my child was no one's business, but people love to be nosy and gossip about others' perceived poor decisions. Later, I discovered that a girl I was once close with at the school had disclosed to my child's father's ex-girlfriend that I was pregnant by the same man she had a child with. At that moment, I realized that people truly do not always have the best intentions for you. They really just enjoy highlighting the drama that doesn't even involve them.

Shortly after my visit to that school, I received a call from another man I had been involved with. He relayed messages from the father of my unborn child's ex, who was spreading rumors about me. She falsely claimed that we were friends and that I had betrayed her trust because she allegedly shared personal details that I had no recollection of ever hearing or discussing with her. At that point, it became difficult to ignore the false narratives being circulated about me, especially because educators who had taught me and known me since childhood were entertaining the nonsense. My emotions began to waver once again. Although I remained far away from the school, I felt as if I needed to defend myself; but instead, I had to bury my emotions. Still, I knew I had to remain level headed despite the negativity surrounding me.

September was coming to an end and my due date was approaching. I had six weeks to figure out a plan for both my children. One of my close friends shared the contact information of a woman who lived in one of our neighborhoods in town and babysat children for a much lower price than daycare. At that moment, I wasn't paying much for Amir, just giving what I could when I could. But with this new woman, I was going to have to pay USD 400 a month—which was fine, considering I'd be working. My rent was USD 725, and although there weren't supposed to be three people living in the apartment, I planned to stay in my one bedroom until Amir turned four, which would be in two years. I just had to remain discreet and out of the way.

Life had been hectic—working multiple jobs and picking up random gigs, whether it was doing hair, babysitting, or helping with odd projects. I was ready to earn a steady and higher income in just a few more months. My child's father had been in consistent contact and agreed to take me to the hospital.

Early in the morning on September 24, 2016, the contractions started to come on strong. Having experienced birth once before, I felt like I was handling things with a bit more ease this time around. I tried reaching out to the father of my child, but his phone kept going to voicemail. I didn't want to rush to the hospital anyway, so I decided to give it some time, since during my last pregnancy I had been turned away because the contractions weren't close enough. I called my sister and she told me to start timing them. All the while, I continued trying to reach out to the father of my child. After several attempts, I was just about to call my sister to come get me when he finally called back. He apologized and asked if it was okay if he still took me. I told him I still needed him and that I would be ready.

On the way to the hospital, even though it had been a while since I'd seen him, it felt like no time had passed. We talked about his past experiences with labor and my own, even sharing some laughs. It was a nice 45-minute drive, and having him there really warmed my heart. Once at the hospital, he stayed with me until I was admitted. He said he had to drop off his daughter at daycare and would be right back. A part of me felt like he was trying to be there for me in private. His energy didn't seem calm—as if he were hiding something. If he had really planned to take me, wouldn't he have arranged for someone else to take his daughter? I ignored the feeling, but deep down I was concerned. Being a father to your child shouldn't cause turmoil. While I was grateful for his presence, I didn't want to implode or explode his life—I just didn't want to have another child with an absent father.

As time passed, I sat alone in the hospital bed, waiting for my second child to be born. Countless thoughts circled my mind: What would my future look like now? Would I be able to handle this responsibility? Surprisingly, I was handling the contractions well.

When the nurse came around for the last time to ask if I wanted an epidural, I finally gave in, unsure of how much longer I would have to wait for my son's arrival.

Around 2 p.m., the contractions became intense, and soon it was time to deliver. My son's father returned just in time to witness the birth. As we waited, I looked over at him and asked if everything was alright. He said yes, just that a lot was going on. Even though I was the one in pain, I couldn't help but be concerned about him. His life was changing, too. I hoped the mother of his daughter would come to terms with this new reality—if she knew. He seemed like he was trying. He asked if I needed anything, offered to get food, and told me to let him know if I needed help. Through the pain, I managed to smile at his effort. It wasn't long before it was time to push.

At 3:09 p.m., after a few pushes, my second born, Tariq, made his arrival—with the cutest shaped head and tiny body. His dad cut the cord, held him, and took several pictures. He smiled, and for a moment, it seemed like he was really bonding with his newborn son.

Every day, he came to the hospital. He brought me food and was attentive to Tariq. When I asked if he wanted to sign the birth certificate, he inquired about the last name. I told him I included both of ours, which he seemed fine with, like he wanted his son to share his name too. After we left the hospital, he brought his mom to my apartment—though she didn't come inside—to see Tariq. He made a few appearances over the following weeks. But then, he disappeared. No returned calls, no texts. He claimed he'd be there, but it looked like I was going to handle everything on my own—which, honestly, I had already mentally prepared for. So I adjusted my mindset once again to endure what was ahead.

Before I returned to work after six weeks, Tariq's dad reappeared. He explained that the mother of his daughter had suspicions and was now placing strict rules on when he could see his daughter. I told him that if she truly loved him and he wanted to be with her, she'd have to accept his newborn son. And there I was—rocking in a chair with one baby nursing and the other tugging at me for attention—consoling a man who hadn't shown up for his son since we left the hospital. For some reason, I always find empathy for those who disregard my feelings and needs.

That same night, we talked on the phone and he came to see Tariq. He asked me for a favor and even showed me around his neighborhood, pointing out where I could find him. In that moment, I was naive and innocent to the ways of people. He came back around so I could help him—but he had no intention of staying. That's when my sweet nature started to turn into rage. I didn't ask him to be here. He came back on his own terms and then had the audacity to walk away from his son without a word.

A tumultuous six weeks passed, and I returned to my job as a teacher assistant. I explained to the principal and my students that I would be leaving soon, as I was actively searching for a teaching position to better support my two children. In my search for a teaching position, I didn't consider the culture of the school or how it could impact my mental health; I focused solely on the fact that I had two babies to support and a roof to keep over their heads. Whoever offered me the job, I was going to gladly accept. I really wanted to become an emotional and behavioral disorder educator, but apparently there were no positions available. More importantly, while I was familiar with the students at the former school where I had worked, I knew I didn't want to work under the man who had once made a teacher cry and consistently agitated other educators. However, if something had been available, I probably would've still worked there.

After submitting countless applications, I landed an interview at a predominantly Black school located in one of the rougher neighborhoods close to my hometown. With a huge smile on my face, I walked into the office and greeted two Black women—one who appeared calm and poised, and another who seemed arrogant and standoffish. The calm one turned out to be the principal, while the arrogant one was the AP. I sensed a very strong negative energy in the room as questions were posed to me. Still, I made sure to stay focused on the positive energy present. The conversation with the principal was delightful as we began to bond over the fact that we both attended Howard University. Unfortunately, the AP seemed impatient and interrupted the conversation, expressing that we needed to move forward with the rest of the interview. She did so in a very passive-aggressive way, which sent a chill through me and caused a sharp pain in my chest. But I needed a job, so I kept smiling as I wrapped up the interview.

Shortly after, I was offered the position—a decision that would ultimately cause waves of emotion, break my spirit, and push me through battles I had yet to experience. I was stepping into an organizational culture that didn't align with the free spirit I embody. The decision to lead a stable life must be made carefully—not carelessly—and in the urgency and pressure to increase my income, I hastily signed a contract. Nothing lasts forever, but for now, I have to do what's best for my children.

3
Navigating intersectionality in a hostile hierarchical culture

Here, I address the challenges of finding stable work in a hostile environment. This chapter describes my experiences in a school where a Black AP created a dictatorial atmosphere, leading to repeated adverse experiences.

Entering a new position as an educator at a Title I school in a troublesome neighborhood, there were many challenges that administration, educators, and parents had to endure. My mindset walking into this new position was to do the best I could, use my passion for improvement to the fullest, and avoid giving anyone in higher positions a reason to harass me. For any job, I value the freedom to do what I need within the required parameters. Walking into a new teaching position feels like a form of hazing. I accepted a role as a first grade teacher, and to create my class, they pulled students from the other first grade teachers; essentially, it felt like I was given the students no one else wanted. While the school was filled with challenging students—some bright, some struggling, and many traumatized—it felt like they gave me the most difficult mix. Because of this, they assigned me a paraprofessional to help manage the behavior issues.

My aide was a tall, Haitian American woman with locs from New York, and our energy blended well, which is crucial when working toward academic and behavioral improvements. My first grade team included four other women: a mixed-race woman with long locs from the Northeast, who, like me, was a Gemini; two other Black women from Florida—one who knew my sister and another who was vibrant, helpful, easygoing, and minded her own business. Last, there was a grumpy, older Jamaican woman next door. She was often out sick, so her attitude didn't bother me much. My empathy allowed me to understand her battles, but I occasionally had to remind her not to project her misery onto me.

I had a class of about nineteen students, roughly half boys and half girls, all ethnic children with varying needs. Every day, I entered the building and went straight to my room, doing my best to avoid the hallways—the school felt heavy on my spirit, almost like a prison. I also did my best to avoid the AP, sensing her snobbish attitude would eventually be a problem. My goal was to make it through six months and, with luck, land the position I truly wanted—teaching in the Emotional Behavioral Disorders (EBDs) classroom.

When walking my class to lunch through the halls, I noticed a few vibrant teachers, but the overall atmosphere was far from cheerful. I knew I was working in a hostile environment, and those never suited me. My team gave tips on minding my business, and everyone mostly kept to themselves. We only gathered for meetings in the team leader's room, then returned quickly to our own. My sixth grade history teacher used to say, "You look good, you feel good"; so, I always dressed up to lift my mood.

Now a mother of two, breastfeeding and exhausted, I didn't want my stress to carry over into my home life. I managed to remain stable for over three years by staying hyperaware of my mood, body, and surroundings. I track when my energy is high, low, or angry. This new position required serious self-awareness. I love children and don't want them hurt or sad, but I've never had much patience for primary students—the noise, the constant correction. Still, even with behavior issues, their innocence pulls at your heart. But the chaos in my class sometimes made me forget they were just little kids.

Only about five of my nineteen students were on grade level. About nine seemed to need IEPs (Individualized Education Program), likely for ODD (Oppositional Defiant Disorder) or OHI (Other Health Impairment). Resolving these issues was tough— their behaviors were intense. Constant tattling, fighting, and one student who harassed others despite being bright. His mother had high expectations, but that didn't stop the behavior. Many girls were sassy and defiant, and one Haitian boy constantly bullied others. Despite the chaos, I knew it was on me to win the kids over and improve outcomes. With help from my parapro-fessional, I believed we could make progress—I just had to stay focused.

After work, I rushed to get my kids, then drove 30–40 minutes home. Since Tariq was born, Amir had become extra clingy and whiny, which triggered me more than ever. I thought the new job would relieve stress due to better pay, but being a single mom to two babies—one breastfeeding and the other emotionally needy—was crushing. One night, I yelled at Amir for crying while I bathed Tariq. I broke down in tears. I felt horrible and exhausted. Still, I had to pull myself together every night to face the next day.

Amir used to sleep in my bed, but now I place Tariq in the crib and Amir on the bed. After they fall asleep, I sneak to the futon couch for a breath of space. A month into the job, my motivation continued but began to dwindle. Being a first-year teacher meant that everyone had something to say. One day, the school counselor gave me unsolicited suggestions in a condescending tone, as if I were a child. I confided in the principal—who was more approachable than the AP—and afterward, the counselor came to my class to apologize.

As distasteful as it sounds, working with Black women often triggers me. I'm unsure if it's our shared struggles or how society shapes us, but I often feel an unspoken tension—an attitude I don't quite understand. There are exceptions—some Black women are warm and easygoing—but too often, there's stand-offishness or aggression. I know my environment affects my demeanor too, so I get it; but I wish we saw one another as allies, not adversaries. Staying in my classroom with minimal interaction preserved some peace.

I managed my class well most of the time, but recess and lunch were chaotic. When structure dropped, so did behavior. I constantly reminded them not to embarrass me in the hallway, which helped with line behavior. Still, I stopped taking my lunch break and began sitting with them in the cafeteria—I couldn't take my eyes off them. It was exhausting, but as a new teacher, people assume you can't handle it. I sensed the AP was warming up to me; I heard her mention to my mentor that I might return the next year. She even complimented my outfits, but her general attitude was not for me. It wasn't just how she treated me but also how she spoke to all the staff: condescending, belittling, full of gestures and sharp tones. I'm highly sensitive to energy, and I saw how others either stayed out of her way or quietly disliked her.

The school's energy was low. If I let it, it would break me. I knew I had to protect my peace—otherwise, I'd risk another hospitalization. And I can't afford to fall apart.

Struggling to manage a class whilst enduring the milestones of my older son Amir was a battle for me. Oftentimes, people would comment on him because he did not talk. However, at home, he would say his letters and sounds and try to read books. Eventually, I reached a point where I wanted to keep Amir away from people to avoid the judgment. Struggling with being a mother and all that it came with—whether it was finances or unsolicited comments—I was bothered. Then, to work at a school that was spiritually draining made me even more exhausted, especially because I was working with high-needs students.

There was this one particular boy, as cute as can be, dressed nicely, with an outgoing personality, but this student struggled academically. I would work on word recognition and letter-sound blending, but by the next day, it was like all that I had taught went down the drain. I made sure I remained in contact with parents because I believe that they are vital to the progress of their child. Unfortunately, when I requested a conference with this student's parent, the dad seemed more mesmerized by me than focused on the point of the conference. I explained to this father what was going wrong and his son's struggles, and he, in turn, started talking about how he teaches his son the importance of keeping his shoes clean.

It was difficult to work with parents who did not see the importance of an education—at least the importance of reading. I was attempting to give some tips and advice, but I drew back when he shifted the conversation to something irrelevant to school. Additionally, I was battling with this student who came to school unkempt almost every single day. He was kind, but other kids would bother him; so oftentimes, he would land himself in a fight.

I am no fan of the system. I do not care for social workers, because plenty of times they would enter a situation automatically with the defense of "the parent is the problem" without utilizing an open heart. However, I felt the way the student was coming to school was concerning, and he was being bullied due to his uncleanness. After a long battle with myself, I finally reported it—not to have him taken away, but for his parents to realize that you cannot send your child off into the world unkempt.

Another student came to school smelling like pee, as if she was sleeping on a dirty mattress in her clothes. She was not a bad student, but battled with a lot of aggression as well as absenteeism. The condition of the previous school I subbed at was minor compared to this school. The battles I witnessed each child fought were horrific, and being the empathetic person that I am, this too began to take a toll on me.

I knew these children had several learning challenges, but their challenges were due to home environments, oblivious parents, and/or negative influences within the school. Battling with the issues of the students while enduring the overall negative atmosphere was challenging.

However, in the midst of the chaos, I found a guy who kept me interested through laughter. As they say, laughter is the best medicine. Although things were not perfect, it was nice to socialize with someone. He had the ability to take my mind off things. He had an excellent sense of humor and, additionally, he was familiar—he was a guy I had known since childhood but hadn't seen since elementary school. We would speak before work, on my breaks, and even after work. The consistency within communication kept me distracted from the hostile environment.

However, the nice distraction did not stop me from being adversely impacted by the hostility. I missed a couple of days due to the trainings that I had to complete. When I returned, I discovered that my paraprofessional had been pulled from my classroom without my being informed. I had been managing the classroom by myself for days without realizing she wasn't there because the class was actually behaving quite well.

One day, whilst I was teaching, my former paraprofessional came to let me know that the AP had pulled her from the classroom. I wasn't entirely upset that she was removed, but I was more bothered by the fact that the AP didn't think I needed to be informed. It showed a lack of consideration, which added more fuel to the fire I already had within.

I am not one to let injustices slide, and I had already felt slighted at the beginning of the year when my classroom didn't have any laptops or tablets while every other class did. It took me saying something to my mentor for each teacher to offer up an electronic item. Other students were receiving their iReady reading and math lessons, whereas I had to pull resources from elsewhere and make do with what I already had. I can say that behavioral problems decreased once I was able to incorporate electronics into my reading and math rotations.

Soon after my paraprofessional told me the news, my chest began to cave in. I was having a panic attack. In the middle of teaching, I asked her to keep an eye on the classroom while I signed out for the day. I needed to leave the school because I felt on the verge of losing all control. As I rushed to the office manager to let her know I needed to go home, she noticed that I was in a crisis and contacted the AP—the last person I wanted to see. The last person.

At that moment, I knew my job was done for because I could not possibly hold back how I felt toward this AP. She was arrogant, inconsiderate, with a major chip on her shoulder. When she sat me down to figure out what was wrong, I explained that I didn't appreciate not being informed about the changes made while I was gone. She told me that I had another paraprofessional assigned to my class, but he had yet to show up.

I also told her she was not a good leader and shared what could have been done differently. By her facial expressions, she felt attacked and responded the only way she knew how—with fake concern and gestures—and asked me if I needed a few days off. I explained that I just needed to go home for the day because of my anxiety. After leaving the office, I immediately grabbed my items from the classroom, hopped in my car, and drove off with the intention of loving on my children even harder once I got home.

I returned to school the next day—better than I was the day before—but not quite with the same spirit I had in the beginning of this new job. The guy they sent to be my new paraprofessional was worse than working with students; it was like having another child in my room. He wanted to play, he wanted to joke, and he was completely unfocused on the purpose of being in my classroom. He would leave the classroom randomly for long periods of time; but honestly, I enjoyed his absence. He caused a shift in my classroom that was unpleasant, which resulted in more disciplining and less teaching. My co-worker has been out a lot lately, and I had some of her students in my classroom today due to the shortage of substitutes. I knew this teacher was ill, but for the life of me I could not understand why she just would not resign. I would never want to spend my last years—or days—in a school that was this unappreciative of me, or even in a school as depressing as this one. I knew that once these few months are up, I must find employment elsewhere. I am just hoping and praying it will be in the EBD classroom at my mom's school. They were currently working under a new principal, and she seemed likable, so the environment might be alright—although I would be returning after hearing a host of rumors about me. However, the one person who was spreading those rumors has since left the school and found employment elsewhere within the district. At this moment, any place would be better than this one—it is literal hell, and I do not know how long I can withstand the heat without exploding.

Every day before lunch, students go to recess. All the first grade students run wild on the playground, and me and the three other ladies on the team sit outside. The older lady usually stays inside, away from all the chaos. It gets so busy outside that I can't necessarily keep an eye on all my students, especially because they're always bunched together. Unfortunately, the playground is on sand and, of course, students sometimes end up throwing it. There was one incident that triggered the AP to approach me in the cafeteria. She talked about how one student had sand in his hair, and like always, she had so much attitude when addressing me. She pretty much implied that I do not watch my students. While I agree that as a parent, I would be upset if my child came home with sand in their hair, I cannot realistically stop a situation like that immediately when there are sixty other students on the playground. As a result, I had to choose to have recess in the back of my classroom, away from other students. It was better, in the sense that I did not have to worry about conflicts with students outside of my class or sand wars. However, I lost the opportunity to have even a second with the other adults to discuss our day or whatever we wanted to talk about. Those 20–30 minutes were essential for my sanity, but I had to remain in isolation due to my students' mishaps.

After a while of dealing with my new paraprofessional, I directed him to leave my classroom and not return. I am still not sure what he did after that, but he never came back. Oftentimes, I took matters into my own hands because I didn't see anyone handling the situations as I felt they should. For example, one day was so horrendous that I called a parent to have him pick up his son, who was bullying and harassing every student in my classroom. I didn't bother to contact the principal—I just made the informed decision to have him removed from school. Luckily, the parent complied. Technically, there are certain protocols for removing students from school that must be followed, but I chose to do my own thing and, fortunately, got away with it. My patience was running thin. I began to question whether I could even handle being an educator at all, especially considering I have my own two children to raise and my own mental struggles. Dealing with several children at once, particularly children with various behavioral issues, causes me to become overstimulated. Once I am overstimulated, I become annoyed and aggravated easily, and as a result, my aggression becomes explosive.

Some weeks were better than others, but I could never seem to have consistent, exceptional weeks at work. Then, when I left work, I had my obligations as a mother. Amir's behavior was regressing. It was as if once Tariq was born, Amir became clingier and whinier. My patience wore thin. If I ever did get to relax, it was only for a few hours before bed. As soon as I began to calm my mind, something else would arise and stress me out all over again. One morning, Amir was extremely whiny and I was running late for work. My elevator was broken, so I had to collapse the stroller and carry all our things downstairs—but Amir was refusing to move. It was like he was tormenting me. I had to place everything downstairs, then return to the third floor to retrieve a screaming toddler. I grabbed him and, completely overwhelmed, lost my mind. I scolded him for behaviors he didn't even understand. Yelling at him was ineffective and pointless, but I needed to release my rage, and I did so on my child—who didn't ask to be here in the first place. Once I made it to my car, I settled into the driver's seat, laid my head on the steering wheel, and sobbed. The hate I felt toward myself and my choices swirled in my mind. I was tired—exhausted—and I didn't know how to cope. After a minute of sobbing uncontrollably, I wiped my face with the back of my hand, put the car in reverse, accepted that I was going to be late, and turned on my music to drown out the chaos in my head.

Living with my highly sensitive nature is extremely difficult in hostile work environments. While I knew this, I still thought I'd be able to handle myself, regardless of what was happening around me. But it is easier said than done. I've tried to avoid encounters with the AP, but if I am late enough, I inevitably have to face her. Every little move I make feels critical, as I try to avoid an emotional explosion. When I first accepted the job, I focused on the fact that the principal and I got along. But in school systems, APs tend to do the bulk of the work—and rarely do principals extend themselves more than the assistants. My sensitive nature pairs poorly with my low tolerance for individuals who abuse their false sense of power. I believe in communal leadership, where everyone works together and all voices matter, rather than individualistic leadership, where those in power push their own ideologies and force compliance.

In addition to the depressive, hostile environment, the Exceptional Student Education (ESE) team was not meeting with students as needed due to being overloaded. Many students in my class needed to be evaluated, but when I met with the ESE support facilitator, she only explained the process vaguely and didn't provide me with a clear direction. So I took it upon myself to create Behavior Intervention Plans (BIPs). When I brought them to her, she explained that I needed to conduct six weeks of data collection first. Although my time was wasted, I discovered I could write up behavioral intervention plans, which gave me more confidence to apply for a position working with EBDs. It might seem unusual that I want to work with students who have EBDs while I'm navigating my own mental health challenges and currently dealing with students who display behavioral issues, but there is a reason behind my desire to do so. I believe I will be good at it because I've been in similar shoes: I know what it feels like to take an exam with overwhelming noise in your head, I know what it feels like to try to calm down after being overstimulated, and I know what it feels like to be misunderstood. I genuinely believe that as I help these students grow, they will also help me grow. Additionally, working with a small cluster of students as opposed to managing a full classroom is a vastly different experience, and I'm hopeful that the overall environment will be more supportive and fulfilling.

The high level of stress I've endured since starting this job has affected me deeply. It even impacted my breast milk production—it started to decrease. On top of that, my older son got sick, and I had to miss several days of work. I hated missing work because students only behaved when I was there; when I was gone, multiple issues would arise. Since Amir started daycare, I've been hypervigilant about his health. The last thing

I wanted was to care for a sick child, especially as a hypochondriac, which only increases my anxiety. Nevertheless, I had to push through with two sick children. I missed Tuesday, Wednesday, and Thursday, and returned on Friday. I had nothing planned, and to make matters worse, I had five extra children in my room because another teammate was out. Then, the AP walked in to do an observation—without notice—just to meet her data quota. My spirit was boiling. She had placed me in an impossible situation, and as she entered, I was stapling math packets for the next week. I ignored her presence; my chest caved in and my ears burned. She noticed I wasn't shifting into "observation mode," so she gestured for me to come over and told me what to do. I simply looked at her and turned away, unwilling to cause a scene in front of my students. I had lost some of my composure, but not all. I knew that the students would mirror me, so I refused to explode in front of them. Later, she told me to see her in her office. I knew what that meant, but I no longer cared about uncomfortable conversations. I was fed up.

In her office, she told me that based on what she saw, she couldn't give me a good observation score. I explained that I had extra students and that I had been out all week with sick children—who were still sick. I had just handed my baby over to my best friend Crystal because he couldn't go to daycare until cleared. I didn't mention my stress or the drop in breast milk, but I did express how overwhelmed I felt. She said she'd return in the afternoon to give me a second chance to correctly complete the observation.

She returned to my classroom that afternoon to conduct the observation again. This time, I leaned into my strengths as an educator—I managed behaviors effectively, delivered the lesson with purpose, and after about 30 minutes, it was over. The tense energy that had been building inside me finally began to fade, and I was able to return to my regular rhythm with my students. After school, I dismissed my students and received an email with the results. When I opened it, I noticed the same feedback from the original observation had been kept, despite the second opportunity to demonstrate improvement. It became clear that the redo had served no actual purpose.

I went to speak with my mentor about it. She explained that based on those marks, I might not be hirable anywhere else in the county. It was devastating to hear, especially as a mother, because it felt like an intentional act to jeopardize the security I was working so hard to provide for my children.

I was overwhelmed with emotion. Frustration gave way to a deep, consuming anger. In that moment, I felt like I had reached a breaking point. My thoughts darkened, and while I didn't want to feel that way, I found myself imagining confrontational scenarios that reflected how powerless I felt. Around that time, my best friend arrived to drop off Amir. I was visibly upset and didn't care who saw. I voiced my frustrations loudly and without restraint. My language was strong, my tone was sharp, and I wasn't trying to hide how overwhelmed I felt. It takes a lot to push me to that edge, but once I'm there, I struggle to hold back—regardless of who's present. At the age of twenty-five, I didn't yet have the emotional tools to process my reactions in a healthy way. On the one hand, some individuals might view my situation as one where I had full control and should have responded more appropriately despite the principal's behavior, but on the other, given the emotional state I was in, I had very little capacity for self-regulation, and I responded the only way I knew how in that moment—by moving in silence. Silence for me has always been the tool I reach for when I feel on the verge of exploding. I have not yet developed strong emotional restraint, but I know that I must learn how to do so sooner rather than later if I am to survive and thrive within the dominant American culture.

This was my first truly demanding job. In the past, I hadn't viewed any job as permanent or defining because I believed I had the freedom to choose my path. But this time was different. I had little ones relying on me. My mother always told me, "No matter what happens, make sure there's a roof over your kids' heads." That's the only thing I was trying to do—hold it all together.

Crystal, my best friend, pulled me aside and gently encouraged me to get into the car. She said, "Buruuj, people can't see you like this." A friend like her is invaluable—she's my balance when I'm unraveling. She has a way of keeping her composure that I've always admired. She sat with me until my emotions settled, then drove me to the back of the school so I could leave discreetly. I wasn't fully calm, but I had regained just enough control to go back into my classroom and gather my things.

The next morning, I woke up with a heavy heart. The weekend dragged on like an anchor, and I knew I had to find a solution if I hoped to transfer to a different school the following year. That night, I had a dream replaying the incident, but with violent imagery that disturbed me. In the dream, I confronted the AP with aggression, and although I felt a strange sense of relief within the dream, it unsettled me when I woke.

It's important for people to understand that some individuals have a harder time enduring negativity, especially when it's persistent, even if indirect. When someone consistently brings an unkind or confrontational attitude into the workplace, it can feel deeply disempowering. In Black American culture, unfortunately, such attitudes have often been normalized, especially in spaces where authority and power dynamics are at play. Many of us grow up learning how to navigate this tension, brushing it off or adapting to survive. But some of us, especially those who are emotionally attuned or highly sensitive, absorb it more deeply. And sometimes, it leads to emotional exhaustion or even thoughts that feel out of character.

This isn't about being unstable; it's about accumulated stress. Prolonged exposure to toxic energy can alter how we think and feel. It might only take one dismissive comment or moment of disrespect to unleash a flood of emotion that's been bottled up for weeks or months. I never acted on my dream, but the fact that such a vision even entered my mind scared me. I couldn't look at the AP without feeling triggered. Love and hate are both deeply intense emotions—and I was swimming in the latter every time I thought of her.

When I returned to school, my mentor called me in for a conversation. She gently suggested I take a personal day to myself, explaining that my temper had clearly reached an unhealthy level. She even asked if I had high blood pressure. I told her no—mine typically runs low. She was surprised, but still advised me to find something calming to do for the day and focus on relaxing my mind.

She also recommended I ask the principal for another observation to ensure I would be eligible for rehire next year. I knew I wouldn't be returning to that school, but I also understood that the AP's feedback had the potential to impact my future options across the county. It felt like a deliberate move to remind me of her authority. I took my mentor's advice and went straight to the principal's office. She agreed without hesitation. The principal was pleasant and respectful, though rarely visible. Most of our daily interaction came from the AP's more abrasive energy.

In many Black communities, there's a perception that it's acceptable to carry yourself with a defensive or aggressive tone—but that doesn't make it right. I look forward to the day when more people, especially in leadership, understand that respect and professionalism should always be the standard.

After leaving the principal's office, I felt lighter. But from that day on, I would continue having vivid dreams involving the AP—dreams filled with anger and confrontation. It took a long time for those thoughts to begin to fade.

On my day off, I decided to relax without my children. I took Amir to daycare and Tariq to his babysitter, stayed home, and drew some bunny rabbits for my school's bulletin board. Artwork always helped calm my thoughts. As I rejoiced in the silence, my heart smiled thinking about how the school year was finally coming to an end. I also sat reflecting on my babies. It seems that as a mother, you crave energy and space to breathe, but once you have that alone time, you begin to miss your children even more. It's a strange dynamic—like saying, "Leave me alone," but also,

"Don't go too far." I started thinking about how I could have handled some things differently, but honestly, I'm glad I said what I needed to say to the principal. I'm glad I expressed how I felt, regardless of how it came out, because at the end of the day, there's a certain level of empathy a person should have when working with others, and she lacked that—as well as professionalism. Professionalism isn't just about wearing a suit or following protocol; it goes deeper than that. We are spiritual beings before we are physical ones, and we often forget about basic human decency and how to approach others. I can rest knowing I'll be okay and that karma handles all things in due time.

Of course, when I returned to school, I spoke with my teammates about the incident, and they expressed their own frustrations because no one really appreciated the AP's attitude. In fact, everyone had recently learned that the principal would be leaving the school, and someone would have to step into her role. I laughed because deep down, I knew—it was obvious— the AP would be the one to step up. Many didn't like the idea of our current principal leaving, and rumors were flying about who would replace her. I didn't worry about it though, because I already knew I wouldn't be returning next year. I had made my distaste for the environment known, and they had decided not to renew my contract. I didn't have a set plan yet, but I knew opportunities would come.

As the school year wound down, the students grew more antsy, and slowly but surely, my mind began to feel at peace. I was planning to work a summer job with a student with autism whom I had worked with before, so I already had a source of income lined up, and I still planned to accept occasional nanny jobs. Not having income is a hard pill for me to swallow. I always needed to know where my next check was coming from, or I'd be overwhelmed with anxiety. I also had a busy summer ahead: a four-day new teacher orientation, taking my general knowledge exam, and completing five gifted education courses. To be more marketable, I figured it was best to become certified in multiple areas. Even though I really just want to teach students with EBDs, I'm not sure if any openings will come up.

On the last day of school, I returned my keys with a mix of excitement and relief, knowing I'd never have to return to the place that almost cost me my well-being. I appreciated the camaraderie among the teachers, but I despised the leadership. In the years that followed, I'd occasionally run into former colleagues who shared how many teachers had left since the AP took over. The school's letter grade had even dropped. It's vital for educators to understand that leadership means creating and maintaining a healthy environment—when staff feel safe and supported, they thrive. Even when they don't agree with decisions, they're more likely to comply if their leader has cultivated a respectful and nurturing organizational culture. It's always a win when your teachers stay, not when they drop off like flies. The ones who remain in toxic environments are either those with strong coping systems who can block out the noise, those who unknowingly contribute to the toxicity, or those unaware of the subtle harm it's doing to their mental health. Many teachers had heard about my conflict with the AP and actually applauded me for standing up. I'm just glad that after I left, others followed suit—on their own terms—which validated that I wasn't the problem. She was. Her karma is managing a school with declining performance and losing valuable staff because she prioritized feeding her ego over creating a supportive environment.

Summer came and went quickly; the pace was nonstop as I tried to line up all my responsibilities. The guy I'd been talking to throughout this time continued to reach out consistently, which I appreciated; it helped to have someone who brought a sense of ease while I was juggling multiple tasks and caring for two children. At the moment, I'm living in a one-bedroom apartment, but the condominium's policy only permits two people to reside in a one-bedroom unit. I'm nervous about the possibility of being forced out; so I decided that by the end of the year, I'd look for a two-bedroom apartment or condo before things escalated. Some neighbors in the community had become increasingly nosey, and the president of the HOA (Homeowners Association) recently questioned me about who was living in the unit. Naturally, I lied. With everything else going on in my life, I didn't need added anxiety stemming from housing concerns.

After attending job fairs and only securing one interview, I finally landed an opportunity for an EBD teaching position at the same school where I previously worked as a paraprofessional and substitute teacher. My mom had recommended me for the role. Although the principal expressed hesitation about hiring family members, she still gave me a shot at the interview. By some stroke of luck, I was hired. She later explained that the hiring was based on a point system, and while another candidate had earned more points, he declined the offer—opening the door for me. She brought me and my mom into her office and explained why she normally doesn't favor having family members work together, and we both assured her that it wouldn't be an issue. My mom, who is a union steward, usually focuses on representing employees and advocating on their behalf. As for me, I've never been the type to stir up unnecessary drama, and my mom typically minds her own business at work. More importantly, if any issues were to arise, I'd handle them myself.

Later, the principal asked to speak with me privately. She told me she had heard stories about my past, specifically involving men I had allegedly been involved with at the school. My chest tightened immediately, and I couldn't help but wonder who brought up my name—and why they felt the need to share that information. It had nothing to do with my qualifications or how I perform my job. Currently, I am quietly seeing someone at this school; but I've kept it private, just like I always do. The only reason people found out about my involvement with the father of my second child was because I became pregnant; otherwise, I would've kept that under wraps as well. There's also another guy at the school whom I had a past with, and unfortunately, he still desires me and has a tendency to talk too much. Yes, perhaps it's not the best decision to get involved with people at work, but in all honesty, I don't go anywhere else—it's just work and home, home and work. Where else am I supposed to meet someone? Regardless, I left the principal's office unsure of how this school year would unfold, but I had a sense that it wouldn't mirror the challenges of my last job. The principal and AP seemed far more approachable and kinder, and my ESE specialist appeared to be an amazing support as well.

4

Navigating in a clan culture with toxic "family" dynamics

This chapter explores my new workplace challenges, where I encountered gossiping older women and the intertwining of my personal and professional life. It delves into the mental battles I faced while trying to escape this toxic environment.

Many people at that school felt like family because I had known them for a long time. My former teacher was next door to me and the guy I was seeing, Derek, was my paraprofessional. While I worked directly with him, I knew how to separate business from pleasure and stayed focused on the goal. That goal was to close the achievement gap between my students with disabilities and general education students. However, Derek tended to joke around too much, even during work hours. I understood humor had its place, but not when I was trying to prove my worth at that school. I was young and had already been prejudged for fraternizing with men at work. Working alongside older Black women, being viewed as young and vibrant, and paired with a young and vibrant man, I knew assumptions would be made. While those assumptions might have been true, people needed to mind their business. Still, I did my best not to let them affect my spirit.

My mission at the school was clear. When working with students with exceptionalities, people made many assumptions about their abilities—even other teachers. That was why I disliked using the word "disability"; it promoted deficit thinking. The former teacher of my students came into my classroom to give me a "heads up." In his own way, he told me not to push the boys too hard. While he had built good relationships with them as a male figure, he had never challenged them; so I dismissed his advice. I was taking a different approach. I wanted to build relationships to inspire growth. My paraprofessional, Derek, told me to listen to other teachers, but he lacked understanding himself; so I ignored him, too. I had to brush off many comments, knowing my vision for my students had yet to unfold. I was working hard to help them grow. Workplace gossip was its own battle. The teacher next door—Derek's godmother—was one of those church-going folks who always gossiped. I tried hard to ignore her because when I left that school pregnant, she was among those talking about me without knowing the real story.

The school's organizational culture felt like a clan—better than a hostile one—but even clans could be toxic families where everyone gossiped. My mother was not like that, and a few others avoided the drama, though some listened without engaging. Regardless, I tried to stay under the radar. I didn't like being the center of attention. I figured if I focused intently on my job, people would forget who I used to be involved with. But the main issue might not have been Derek's godmother; it could have been the former guy I had messed with, Jason, who worked as a custodian. He still had feelings for me. We were cool then, but I was no longer interested. We had a fling; he was kind and caring, but I knew it was best to remain friends. Still, I knew he might have been watching my moves. People loved reading body language, and in that culture, they often made assumptions about who was into me, especially when I was around men. I had just come back, and Jason told me that Derek's godmother had warned him to stay away from me and that she planned to speak to Derek to do the same.

What bothered me was how she painted me as a predator, as if those men couldn't make their own decisions. Why couldn't she talk to me directly instead of assuming I was some promiscuous woman sleeping with every man I met? Despite her opinion, I treated men well. Unfortunately, they were often the ones who couldn't offer what I wanted. Either way, I was there to work and make a difference. I had two children at home depending on me, and I was a young woman simply trying to figure life out. I didn't need or welcome outside noise that had nothing to do with my mission.

On my first day of teaching, my paraprofessional, Derek, was abruptly snatched out of my room while I was teaching; to this day, I was never told why. Although I wasn't told, I knew why. I worked with fourth and fifth grade boys—aggressive boys—so they paired me with Derek because he was male but later decided to place another female in my room. At that time, I was immediately annoyed because I didn't want to get to know the new female, but it turned out to be the best decision that could've been made. I'm sure someone gave the principal a heads up about Derek possibly fraternizing with me, so she made the safe decision to remove him. However, it could've been done at the end of the day and in a more professional way with some forewarning. I had created a sign for his area and had to redo it to match the new paraprofessional; so I was more annoyed because it ruined what I had already set up. Personally, the principal should've known better than to place a man with me if she was concerned about dating in the workplace, given my history. Other than the sudden removal of my paraprofessional, I already felt comfortable and knew I was right where I needed to be. I was working with nine boys, and it was like I saw myself in each of them. One student loved to escape into his art and became upset when he had to work. Another was an eloquent speaker, quite gifted in talking trash. One loved math and solved problems quicker than anyone else. Two boys were like best friends and talked too much—one was way more sarcastic than the other—and both were into a character from "Five Nights at Freddy's." One student was icy around the edges but could be silly at times. Another was bubbly and talked really fast; most times, he was a delight. One was just very quiet, sweet, but a little sly. Then there was a student many people in the school didn't like, but whom I adored. He struggled with reading and was emotionally and mentally delayed, likely the result of being born to a crack-addicted mother. He had many idiosyncrasies, but he was brilliant in many ways. He knew how to cook, bake, and create things. People didn't see what I saw, but I made sure to protect who he was with all my heart.

Working with students with severe emotional and behavioral disorders comes with many challenges. I may have had a good first week, but the temperaments began to reveal themselves shortly after. Still, it was better to manage nine students than nineteen. I implemented a system where students worked to earn a break. I had to adjust the system frequently because some students wanted computer time but didn't know how to transition back to work afterward. Early on, I openly shared my diagnosis with my students so they wouldn't feel alone, and to show them that despite having the same symptoms they had, I showed up every day and overcame my own challenges. On open house day, I explained my "why" to the parents, and they appreciated knowing a teacher who truly understood their child would be teaching them. However, this also created a dynamic where parents felt they could reach out to me at all hours with personal problems involving their children. A few times, parents were on the phone crying and pleading. It took me a while to realize that if a child has an EBD, nine out of ten times, the parent likely does too. As an empath, I lacked boundaries during my first year and responded too quickly and too often to their needs.

At work, I found so much joy in teaching that I would often escape into the moment, sometimes not even noticing if an adult had walked in. Once, my principal completed an informal observation and left a note on my desk about how much she enjoyed seeing my passion. I hadn't even realized she had come in—thankfully, I wasn't doing anything unproductive. This was the kind of job I wanted, where the administrators were active and supportive rather than working against you. The ESE specialist enjoyed reading my IEPs because I wrote narratives that described the students vividly. I felt appreciated at this school. While there was occasional gossip about my personal life and people clearly watching my interactions with male colleagues, it was easy to ignore at first; but over time, it became more unbearable.

Being a dedicated educator and hard worker, you're almost always overworked and overused. At this job, I wouldn't say I was undervalued, but as the year progressed, more pressure was placed on me because one of the other EBD teachers wasn't pulling her weight. In reality, the other two teachers simply didn't work as diligently. Derek worked with a young White woman who taught the third and fourth grade cluster, and there was an older Black woman who taught the K–2 cluster. It became obvious that they both lacked certain skills. The teacher Derek worked with was dishonest and frequently absent; so when she missed school, I had to take on more students. When new students enrolled, they were placed in my class because of the strength of the partnership between me and my paraprofessional. At first, I was a team player, but as time went on, it became extremely frustrating. I started with nine children and ended with thirteen, teaching three grade levels. When people know you're good, they place more pressure on you, and you really don't have much choice but to comply or quit.

When new students arrived, some of the original students became jealous because they wanted my attention to themselves. As a result, they would act out to get a reaction from me. At the beginning of the year, I explained to my students that just like they had triggers, I did too. I told them I worked hard to create the art in our classroom, so not to touch or damage it. While most of my decorations stayed intact throughout the year, some students were bold enough to destroy a few things. I can honestly say my students brought out the best and worst in me—they helped me recognize areas I still needed to grow. I also explained to them that if they got into trouble inside the classroom, we might be able to work it out together, but if they got into trouble outside the classroom, I wouldn't be able to influence how the consequences were handled. We had a point system in our room, and students received rewards based on their level. When they reached level 3, they were allowed to attend a general education class. If they got into a fight or did something extremely offensive, they were placed on a level freeze. My para and I had to keep daily point sheets and send home daily behavior notes.

Oddly, with all the chaos that surrounded me, one would think that it would have caused me to become overstimulated often; but it came to a point that the chaos became a norm for me and without it, it felt abnormal. As I was driven by my students' motivation, every once in a while a bug—that bug being Jason—was in my ear, telling me what someone had said about me. He was a massive instigator, attempting to pull out information about Derek and me, but I refused to give in to him. I had worked at this school before, but never thought about how heavy the gossiping was because I had not been around to listen. Another paraprofessional came into my classroom to talk to my paraprofessional about someone else's business, and I was taken aback because she was recalling details of someone else's life and knew names. I kept to myself as I tried to focus on planning for the next day. I briefly interjected and told her that I just could not believe she remembered all that—I could barely remember my name.

Working within the K–12 system, I found myself surrounded by small-minded people who could not do anything but talk about other people. Then there were the ones with average minds who talked about average events; very rarely was I surrounded by people who formulated ideas. I did my best to stay in my own lane and away from the gossipers, but when I did step out of my classroom, I managed to maintain my vibrant smile and energy. At times, it was exhausting—being in meetings where conversations always were too extensive, with a lot of complaining occurring. Also, people constantly interrupting my classroom as if I did not have to teach was quite annoying, too. It had gotten to a point where I had to place a sign on my door letting people know not to bother me until my students were on a brain break.

I felt as if they had less respect for my group of students due to them being an EBD cluster, but they needed to take a test like everyone else and deserved the same amount of respect as their general education peers—because they did not interrupt general education classrooms as much as they interrupted mine. The only thing I truly enjoyed about my job was being in my classroom, teaching students who understood me as I understood them.

The first half of the year seemed to fly by, with some hiccups here and there, several phone conversations with parents, and heightened students. Working in a clan culture with a Black family toxic dynamic had its pros and cons—it was like where on one end, there was a commonality, but most individuals within this culture were conditioned to certain behaviors. And when you were someone who had elevated past enduring certain toxic dynamics, you could be perceived as thinking that you were better than everyone else; but in reality, you just wanted to maintain mental peace. It was like within the Black American culture, where one must always carry around this poker face and endure the rattling of one's chains without being bothered. It was unsettling because some would never truly understand how walking around with a mean face, gossiping, and always-on-edge mentality impacted us as a whole. It impacted the subconscious and our overall well-being. As a result, I did my best to embody optimism and happiness, but it did not always exude due to the hearsay that I at times could not ignore.

By the time spring rolled around, I had reached thirteen students, the fights had gotten worse, and my nerves were bad. There was another teacher who could have taken on more students, but they felt I, along with my para, was a stronger fit; they actually removed some students from her class and placed them into mine without taking any of my students away. When the AP would let me know of changes, they knew I was irritated because I would walk away silently, without a word or acknowledgment. The good thing about this job was that they respected my silence and did not nag or force conversations when I was not in the mood. My paraprofessional and my behavior tech used to tell me that they would notice a shift in my energy when I wore all black. I never thought about how I dressed until they pointed it out. Being someone with a very raw and authentic energy was difficult because I could not hide my feelings—I did not know how to walk around with a façade. I could either push things out of my head to ensure I was in a good mood or allow everything to get to me, causing a complete shift in my energy, and everyone would take notice because I was normally a bubbly, vibrant person. My goal anywhere I worked was to keep myself in check because I did not want anyone to see me in a state that would trigger more gossip. I felt more unsafe around uneducated Black people, rigid and uppity White people, and police officers when

I was in a manic state or a state of absenteeism, where I was taken by the spiritual world. In the Black community, there was an increased stigma around severe mental illness; oftentimes, people did not like to talk about their problems. When someone lost themselves, they were ridiculed behind their back with no real support offered. They either felt like you should be saved by Jesus or read the Bible because they had very little understanding of the spiritual realms and trauma itself.

Unfortunately, the invitation of scrutiny soon reached me shortly after a nearby school shooting occurred on February 14, 2018, killing seventeen people that triggered an out-of-body experience within myself. The day I found out, I was startled because my former teacher worked at that school. I found out he was safe, but I was distraught. Apparently, in that school year, 2017–2018, several shootings occurred across the nation, but I was unaware because I did not watch the news. I refrained from it due to my highly sensitive nature—but this time, it hit home and I could not ignore it.

Additionally, Derek viewed me as a nut and did not understand what was going on. The second day after the shooting, I could not sleep at all; I felt spirits awaken me all through the night. I had no clue how I was going to maneuver the workplace, but I decided to write a letter to the principal and AP to explain what I was going through. The spirits told me to complete a fast for seventeen days without food—just water—to purify the seventeen lost souls.

During this time, the only thing I could do was teach. My students were even a lot calmer during this time. When someone was in my class whom I did not want there, they would tell them to get out. Although it was not their place and it was deemed rude, my kids did not have any couth; so they said what they wanted, whenever they wanted. My paraprofessional took the students to lunch for me during this time because she knew I could not be around several energies. Luckily, the principal, along with everyone else, gave me my space—and that was the benefit of the clan culture. I was not sure if others were judging me, but at that moment, I did not see people or pay attention to people—everyone just kept their distance.

I later found out that the one person who did a lot of judging was the one with whom I was intimate with—Derek. He called me crazy and talked about me in a way I would not have expected because I never disclosed our relation to anyone; I thought that if anything, we were friends. During my fast, he saw more than the others at work because he would come to my house, complain about my absenteeism, and say we needed space. I did not care in that moment because I was captivated by the spiritual realm—my focus was on my fast. As days went on, people inquired about my health, but I ensured them that I was alright. The fast itself was peaceful; during that time, my students were the calmest they had ever been, and they understood me more than everyone else. Kids are closer to the spiritual realm—their lives have not yet been interrupted by their ego. Therefore, they sensed what I needed from them before I knew what I needed: a calmness to help me navigate this journey without being overstimulated. However, while the fast was calm itself, storms arose after the fast reached completion.

After I completed my fast, I returned to myself; well, sort of. After feeling spiritually high, I found my way to an excruciating low. I was on edge more than ever. I discovered that Derek had been seeing someone else the whole time and had lied about it. All I had wanted was honesty. To add insult to injury, he intentionally ignored me at school, making it obvious that something had gone on between us. He refused to communicate with me; during this time, he began talking about me, which caused others to speculate, drawing more attention to me than I ever wanted.

One day, I walked into school upset, not because of Derek but because I had spent the entire morning in the hospital with my young son, who had woken up in the middle of the night unable to breathe. He had gone to bed with what I thought was a mild cough and stuffiness. I panicked because I couldn't take him to the hospital myself, so I called 911. Apparently, he had asthma, according to the doctors, who tried placing him on a breathing treatment. After spending all morning at the hospital, I found myself crying profusely; I was just tired of doing everything alone, especially when it came to sickness and ailments.

However, everyone at the school assumed my attitude had something to do with Derek. So, Jason interjected and told me to change myself because people were talking, saying I was upset due to a breakup with Derek—which was entirely untrue. I was filled with rage. I told Jason to stop telling me things and to stay out of my business. I exploded on him like I never had before. In the days that followed, I found myself having a panic attack at work. I asked my behavior tech to get me out of my classroom because I was having uncontrollable movements in my body— jerks in my arms and pain on the left side.

As I waited in the clinic, the staff took it upon themselves to call the emergency room, which I did not want. I didn't want the bill, nor did I care for doctors. Unfortunately, I had no control over the call, and at that moment, I felt embarrassed because everyone saw me in such a vulnerable state. I didn't want the fake concern and didn't want anyone knowing the challenges I faced. It was always odd to me how people would surround you in times of "need" as if they cared; sometimes, those same people were the ones who broke you. I always talked about the importance of treating people right because you never know what they're going through, but that mindset was not commonly applied in the workplace.

My first school year as an EBD teacher was tumultuous, especially when my personal life once again collided with my professional one. People like me were often expected to be doped up on medication and placed in situations where we were cared for rather than allowed to be self-sufficient. Research suggested that we benefited from working on farms or in natural environments; I agreed with that to an extent. However, at that time, I couldn't pursue a career in that space and I certainly wasn't going to allow my life to be reduced to medication and long-term care under someone else's control. As difficult as it was to ride the waves of life alongside people who neither thought like me nor understood me with any real acceptance, I continued to navigate those spaces in the best way I knew how, hoping that over time, the journey would become less burdensome.

That year also added another layer to my already messy personal life, since I kept meeting people through work—mainly because I didn't go anywhere else. While I was capable of handling separation from people, the real issue arose when others didn't know how to manage situations privately or with integrity. On top of that, there were new staff members who knew nothing about me but still felt entitled to comment on my life, often treating it as a source of entertainment. The people I appreciated most were my principal, AP, and the ESE specialist, because they recognized my work ethic and never contributed to the gossip that surrounded me. Their support made my decision to return for another year much easier. I was extremely proud of surviving a full school year—it hadn't been the easiest, but it certainly hadn't been the worst.

I had found my footing that first year as an EBD educator. My kids had grown quite a bit, and students who weren't used to working hard had started putting in the effort. There had been several behavioral challenges, but we overcame them. The greatest accomplishment was watching my students graduate as they moved on to middle school. Some of my students had moved away, new ones had rolled in, and some had stayed but just in a different grade level.

During the 2018–2019 school year, I had a girl in my class. Usually, a girl with behavioral and emotional issues was ten times worse than boys, behavior-wise. Then, a student known for being very boisterous joined my class—he had been extremely disrespectful, and somehow, I had to make a difference in his life. I had always been up for the challenge, but this child triggered me in a whole new way.

A young boy I had taught at the end of my first year in third grade returned as a fourth grader. He had been a smart kid but hated math. The previous year, he didn't even take the math state assessment. Also that same year, he had been involuntarily committed to a psychiatric facility, and his parents were livid. I, too, had become emotional because I hadn't been around when it happened and had to speak with the parents. I had been involuntarily committed on several occasions myself and had not had the best experiences, so I felt for him. Since that incident, I had made sure to protect him from anything like that ever happening again. I chose to endure whatever he put me through because taking a child without parental consent felt gruesome and immoral to me.

There was one new kid, unfamiliar to me but who had already attended the school the year before. He was between foster homes but still seeing his mother. He wasn't a terrible kid with extreme behavioral issues, but those issues were present. This school year, I had accepted that my class size would constantly shift—because that's just how it went. Also, the two teachers I had worked with were no longer working with me. The new third and fourth grade cluster teacher came with a different set of issues that I didn't care for; for the most part, I did a better job at ignoring them.

The beginning of the school year was always the most exciting as I set up my classroom to match the school's theme. Over the summer, I had adjusted to my new norm without Derek around and tried to ignore the fact that I would be returning for another year at the same school as him. Rumor had it that he would be leaving soon, which felt like a relief. But now another issue had arisen—there was a new PE (physical education) coach at the school. Yes, he was attractive, and once again, I knew I'd be a target. I told myself not to even speak to the guy because I didn't have time for drama or gossip.

Over the summer, I had begun practicing gratitude heavily, which shifted my perspective a lot. I started appreciating everything and saw blessings in situations that didn't go my way. At the beginning of the year, Derek's godmother called me into her classroom to apologize after discovering that her godson had ended up with a woman who had, I believe, four or five kids. She said she was disappointed. I found it ironic that she had tried to protect him from me because I had two children, yet he had chosen to be with someone with more. Honestly, the girl was a better fit for him—he was nowhere near my spiritual, mental, emotional, or intellectual level. Still, I hadn't liked how things ended. He acted as if I had done something to him. But it was a new school year and I had put it behind me, hoping everyone else had either forgotten or would leave me alone about the situation.

Additionally, I felt like I had gained a certain level of respect due to my accomplishments with my students. Teachers who had been working for over twenty-five years had never seen an ESE teacher move students academically the way I did. Even my own mother had believed students with exceptionalities were incapable of learning; so she and many other educators were grateful for what I brought to the table. The only issue they had was not minding their business when it came to my personal life. I was young and free, but also dedicated and hardworking. No one who came across me left without gaining a wealth of knowledge or a better understanding of themselves. I wouldn't say I never committed any wrongdoings, but I had an authentic character and a high level of self-awareness, so I often shared my wisdom with those around me.

I tried to be cordial with everyone at the school, though there were some I didn't associate with too closely. One woman at the school was bothered by my honesty. She once called me and asked why I didn't talk to her much. I told her it was because she gossiped too much and I didn't want to be around that energy. Before sharing what I felt, I had warned her that I didn't want to say anything offensive, but she insisted. When I told her the truth, she got upset. She lied a lot and gossiped constantly. That kind of energy weighed on me. I didn't necessarily judge people as good or bad, but that kind of character flaw triggered me.

That first year back at school, I had learned who "my people" were and who to keep things light with. I had also learned that no one could be fully trusted. I knew who the nurturing "mamas" were, who the gossiping "aunties" were, and who the "like-minded" folks were. I decided I would navigate the place accordingly so I could keep my mental health intact throughout the school year. As long as I did my job effectively, I felt I would be alright—these were my thoughts.

With Derek's godmother apologizing, others gone, and my work ethic speaking for itself, the year started off pretty well. The new coach was outgoing, but I made sure to stay in my lane because rumors would certainly surface. This was the year I focused more on publishing my first book about my story of battling mental health. That publication turned out to be a success, and many people supported me—more than I expected. I was proud of myself, and it felt like my life was on an upward trajectory, with more blessings ahead. There's always sunshine with a rainbow at the end of every storm.

People often asked how I managed to write a book, take care of my children, and work at the same time. I didn't know exactly how, but I just knew I had a gift for writing. That was something wonderful about me. I could escape into my mind and write for hours without interruption. It came more easily to me than it did for others, and it didn't take much effort to complete tasks. However, as an educator, the ability to escape into my mind sometimes became an issue because I needed to pay attention at all times. I struggled to focus, especially when the information being presented felt useless or insignificant. Still, escaping came in handy when I needed to ignore certain student behaviors.

This year, the behaviors weren't as bad as the year before, but they were still present. The boisterous student sometimes made it hard to teach, but other times, he managed to display acceptable behavior. The one young girl often eloped—leaving the classroom without permission—and ran around the school doing inappropriate things, then blamed the teachers when she got hurt.

The first half of the year flew by, as I was much more involved in after-school activities. I met a guy whom I helped with his grad school classes, which reignited my own interest in pursuing grad school. I was actively promoting my book, and I met a female colleague at the school who was just as ambitious as I was. She would come talk to me during her break, and we shared our stories and perspectives. We motivated each other in a place where many people were set in their ways and didn't believe in greater possibilities.

Although the beginning of the year flew by, it was hectic with several student elopements and drama involving parents. By the time Thanksgiving break rolled around, I was more than ready for winter break. When I returned, the principal asked me what I had done because three of my most challenging students were no longer enrolled at our school. In my head, I thought, "That's just the universe doing its work." While I understood my students' issues, I too had struggled greatly; at times, it became overwhelmingly difficult.

One of the students who left was the young girl whose mother had tried to make claims against our staff and who had no control over her daughter. Another was a student experiencing severe emotional challenges, constantly moving through foster care and bouncing back and forth between homes, which caused his behavior to worsen.

Although I usually liked finishing the school year with students to reflect on their growth, I needed the relief, especially with state testing approaching. Some of my toughest students were still there, but they were evolving, and it showed.

This year ended on a good note. One of my students went from scoring two Level 1s in math and reading to achieving two Level 4s. A student who had previously hated math and refused to take the test in third grade received a high Level 2 on the math assessment—just three points shy of a Level 3. Other students earned Level 3s on their assessments. These were the kinds of students many teachers considered extremely difficult and not capable of growth or high achievement scores.

The 2018–2019 school year was mildly hectic, especially since my paraprofessionals changed three times. In the end, the person who worked with me didn't know how to effectively discipline, but she did know how to teach, which was helpful for some of the students I didn't always connect with. I managed to keep my distance from the new coach to avoid gossip, and I also kept my distance from Jason, who seemed to watch my every move.

Most individuals at the school eventually came to understand me and knew how to approach me. I was inspired by a colleague and friend to start a motivational clothing line. Maneuvering through this sphere had not been easy, but I felt like I had finally found my footing and continued to grow in my aspirations.

―――――――――――――――――

During the summer, I returned to work at a summer camp as an ESE support staff member. Initially, the camp supervisor and I had a good relationship, but that changed when she realized I was someone who advocated strongly against injustice. The camp had a close-knit "clan-like" culture, and the supervisor often shared personal issues with me. Though she could be dramatic at times, I generally enjoyed the position because it gave me a break from teaching and was only temporary. Most counselors were former campers and my supervisor had been with the city for years.

That summer, my child also attended the camp, and I was told by multiple counselors that the camp lead had been vaping in the presence of children—on buses and even in classrooms. I received a photo confirming this. As a parent, I was alarmed, not only for my child's safety but for all children present. I raised the issue with my supervisor, but she became defensive, as she had known the lead since childhood. I chose to resign, believing the situation hadn't been properly addressed, and requested to be paid for the work I had done. I stood by my decision and did not return. What could've been resolved calmly escalated due to the supervisor's dismissal of serious concerns.

When I am highly distressed, I've learned to rely on healthy coping strategies like meditation, solitude, and reflection. I always evaluate how I respond to situations and consider ways I might improve. However, when it comes to what I view as injustice, especially when it involves my children or my ability to provide for them, I struggle to remain emotionally detached. Life outside work added emotional pressure, but I remained committed to my responsibilities. Ideally, leaders should foster inclusive, supportive environments, but not everyone is equipped to do so. Despite challenges, I continued to grow, learning to walk away from situations that no longer served me.

The 2019–2020 school year brought added pressure. I was working overnight at Amazon, attending graduate school, and supervising aftercare. I was transparent with my students, letting them know I had multiple responsibilities and needed their cooperation. Still, I often felt like my income wasn't enough, no matter how hard I worked. Managing finances, childcare, and my own well-being was difficult. I only maintained the overnight job for three months before I recognized that it was impacting my mood.

Living with a mental health condition meant I had to be extremely mindful of my stress levels and emotional triggers. I had chosen not to rely on medication due to side effects and instead focused on holistic strategies to maintain balance. Juggling parenting, work, and school alone was incredibly difficult, but I remained determined.

That year, I was assigned to the same student for the third consecutive year—a student who struggled deeply with math. I believe it's rarely ideal for students or teachers to remain paired for too long. Frustration can build on both sides. I tried to transition him into more general education settings because he was capable, but the move didn't last. I also began working with a new female student who was often absent and experiencing symptoms consistent with mania. Initially, I was told she couldn't read, but I discovered that she was able to—scoring a high Level 2 on her iReady. With mental health challenges like hers, abilities can fluctuate. On some days, students may perform at high levels, and on others, they may not be able to focus at all. People often overlook this variability.

Another student I supported was quiet and reserved but occasionally displayed unpredictable and concerning behavior. There was a point where he attempted to physically confront me, though he was unsuccessful. Eventually, he was moved to a behavioral school, where the entire school was filled with students who had severe mental health disorders. I've always struggled with the idea of placing students in separate schools because it can feel like giving up on them. Grouping students with complex behavioral and emotional needs together doesn't always result in better outcomes; it can amplify challenges. Families and educators often feel overwhelmed and out of options, which is heartbreaking. Though I felt I wasn't making progress with that student, and it saddened me, I knew it was beyond my control.

Midway through graduate school, I decided I wanted to pursue a PhD. I enjoyed my coursework and felt motivated by my progress. A professor told me about a grant-funded program I could apply for. Regardless of the outcome, I knew further education was the right path for me. I also sensed that my time as an EBD educator was coming to a natural end. Many of the students I had connected with were moving on to middle school. My principal was supportive when I informed her that I might become a full-time student. When I spoke to my ESE specialist, she suggested I take on a new role as an ESE support facilitator—less classroom management and more student pull-outs. The caseload would be larger, but the daily intensity would be lower. I felt appreciated, and after considering it, I accepted the role for the following year because it aligned better with my needs and well-being.

I've always had a strong sense of when my time in a space has run its course. While many see me as personable and kind, I know that under extreme pressure and in negative environments, I can become emotionally overwhelmed. I strived to leave every place on good terms, but sometimes circumstances prevented that. I wasn't rehired at my first job, and although that hurt, I understood my triggers and accepted when it was time to move on. Emotional regulation is crucial for me, especially to avoid being placed in secluded environments that could further impact my health. I've had to walk away from many situations without closure, but I've learned to protect my peace. I always worked to build new skills so I could remain flexible. I never looked down on any job—I just needed a way to support my family. I even considered becoming a plumber or handywoman. Ideally, the best environment for me is one with minimal chaos and lower stimulation.

When the school year ended early due to the COVID-19 pandemic, it felt like a much-needed pause. I had reached a breaking point with a student I'd taught for three years, and we had a difficult moment right before schools closed. Fortunately, other teachers intervened, and I was able to walk away without further conflict. Despite the ups and downs, the student still considered me one of his favorite teachers and continued to ask about me at other schools. That's the complexity of working with children—sometimes, the most challenging ones form the deepest bonds.

During the pandemic, I lived with my mom, my two children, and a puppy while saving to buy a house. I had hoped to move out within a year, but tensions rose quickly, especially with more family members returning home during lockdown. I grew up in a household with many siblings, and while this situation had fewer people, I still struggled with the lack of personal space.

Around this time, I became closer to a colleague—Coach. We were both ambitious, and I appreciated that about him. While I was mindful of professional boundaries, we supported each other's ideas and energy. He encouraged me to start delivering groceries, and I eventually took on multiple side jobs—working for Amazon, grocery shopping, and teaching virtually. Some weeks I made USD 1,000 just from deliveries. I was doing everything I could to provide and secure a home.

Initially, the school year ended on a positive note—I was finally able to separate from students, which gave me the space I had been needing. But as summer arrived, I began slipping into a difficult emotional state. I found myself withdrawing, even from my own children. I didn't want to be touched, spoken to, or even bothered. I felt emotionally overwhelmed and disconnected from everything around me. The constant stream of distressing news about COVID-19 only intensified my feelings. The world felt chaotic, people seemed to be operating out of fear rather than logic, and I was living in a house that was far too crowded for my comfort and peace of mind.

All I wanted was stability—a home of my own—and I began putting intense pressure on myself to make it happen immediately. I was rushing through time, losing sight of how important it was to slow down and give myself grace. My mental state began to spiral. I held onto a lot of frustration and pain, especially toward the fathers of my children, whose absence felt intentional and heavy. Those emotions overwhelmed me, and I found myself sinking deeper into hopelessness. I was emotionally exhausted and questioning everything. It was a time when I felt like I was carrying far more than I could manage, and I struggled to see a way forward.

Summer did not go well. I made money, but I lost my sanity and became disheartened by the fact that we were beginning the school year via distance learning. I wanted my life back to normal. I was starting online as an ESE support facilitator, never having met my pull-out students in person—and this is how we started. A couple of months in, educators returned to school, but students were still attending virtually. On top of that, Amir had to attend classes virtually as well and was not doing well.

I decorated my classroom regardless of whether kids were in attendance and tried to find some peace, even though I was still living in my mother's house. I had no luck finding a home in the county I lived in. Everything was ridiculously expensive, and my debt-to-income ratio was too high. I was working ridiculously hard—and for what? To not be able to buy a house?

To add to the tumultuous waves I was already navigating, I discovered that my dad was suffering from ALS (amyotrophic lateral sclerosis). That revelation heightened my stress and anxiety. The family went to see him when we weren't sure what was going on. He was extremely skinny and could barely move. He had hidden his condition from us for a while. He refused to go to the doctor because he didn't trust them, so he did what he knew best—healed through fasting. Eventually, his parents convinced him to go to the hospital to receive a diagnosis. He ended up on a breathing tube because the main issue was that he could no longer breathe on his own. Never in a million years did I think I'd see my father in such a vulnerable state.

In 2018, after completing my seventeen-day fast, I had received spiritual messages about 2020 and how we were going to lose a lot of people. I couldn't function because I kept wondering if my father was going to be one of them. Trying to buy a house, worrying about my dad, and managing the chaos of COVID-19 kept me in a constant state of panic. In hindsight, it was probably best that students weren't physically in front of me, but a part of me longed for their presence so I could feel like something—anything—was still normal.

I had met a guy at one of my summer jobs who treated me well. When I was emotional, he comforted me, and I was grateful to have someone to lean on; but even that didn't quiet the unsettled feelings inside me.

For the spring semester, parents had the option to send their children back to school. Many were still fearful, but the kids came back. The fall semester dragged on as I continued my PhD courses, which were also disheartening. Starting classes online and not being able to meet my classmates was not fun. I enjoyed personal interactions, and virtual learning lacked the warmth I craved.

While COVID-19 made some people more appreciative and compassionate, it didn't change the attitude of some educators one bit. The gossip continued. The watching eyes didn't stop. And that school year, because Coach and I were actual friends, he began coming around to my classroom more and we socialized more. We got along well because of our mindset. But with someone like me, older women in the workplace were always going to assume the worst. One educator even told me to stay away from Coach. I was bothered by the comment, especially when she later acted like she hadn't said it.

Meanwhile, I was trying to buy a house, stressed about countless things, and had a man of my own—yet people still chose to focus on my personal life. What added fuel to the fire was when Coach came to me and told me that the very same teacher who had once apologized for prejudging me was now stirring up more drama. She had brought up my name to another woman who knew Coach, as if we had something going on. The worst part was that he was married; so, gossiping about him was even more harmful to him than to me. The noise got too loud. I started to see myself become destructive. And without hesitation, I knew—this was going to be my last year at that school.

I had tolerated four years. I think I did well. I reached out to one of my professors so I could become a full-time student. I wasn't part of the grant program, so I just enrolled as a standard PhD student. There were graduate assistantships I could apply for. Yes, my income would decrease significantly, but my peace of mind was more important.

Toward the end of the year—which was dreadful—Derek's god-mother came to me to express how much she appreciated all the work I had done over the years. She told me that no one had ever done what I did at the school. Then she asked why I had to leave. In my head, I thought, *You're part of the reason I'm leaving.* While others could tolerate the toxic behavior and gossip, I could not. It disrupted my energy.

The best part of that school year was finally signing for a house and leaving on a good note. I had no animosity toward anyone, just fatigue from all the extra noise caused by gossip about me. In 2021, I decided to release my second book, which shared the trauma I experienced during my pregnancy and my thoughts about the workplace I was leaving. Yes, it included stories deeply rooted in pain and mental health struggles, and yes, some peo-ple were offended. But I stood by my truth.

Unfortunately, the book became more intriguing because of the drama, and many missed the point. Some people, including Derek's godmother, had their egos bruised because they wanted to be perceived as good people. The truth hurt. She eventually stopped speaking to me when I visited the school, but I didn't concern myself with her feelings. My story was bigger than her.

Working in a clan culture might seem ideal, but when it includes a toxic family dynamic, the joy of working in that environment disappears. Some people avoid family cookouts for that same reason. Sure, we all shared the same vision and passion for the school, but jealousy and attitude wove themselves through the fabric of that place. I felt those energies deeply. Like many Black American families, you always encounter that cousin or auntie who doesn't truly wish you well—and wonders how you made it through the fire.

Still, I was forever grateful to my principal. She gave me a shot and was never the source of my frustration. Someone like me can't peacefully maneuver through just any workplace, but she gave me a stable home for four years—and for that, I was grateful.

5

Forced into a hostile hierarchical culture: Navigating new challenges

In this chapter, I recount my final experiences within a school district, detailing how I was ultimately pushed out due to my belligerent behavior triggered by forced conversations with the principal.

As COVID-19 was still a topic of conversation and had changed the face of education—many were fully remote and numerous jobs had opened up remotely—I was navigating the space within higher ed as a full-time student with an assistantship. I worked alone, spent most of my time handling emails, and rarely spoke on the phone. For the first time in a while, I finally felt a strong sense of peace. There really wasn't any organizational culture to endure because I worked in isolation, away from people. Yes, I found a house in West Palm Beach, even though I was originally from Broward County where my kids attended school. But my assistantship required me to work in Miami-Dade County, so I had to travel through three counties at least three days a week. Still, I didn't mind—it was worth it to be free of people. After years of working in large, overstimulating environments, I realized I couldn't endure being around large groups of people for too long. I needed silence. Silence gave me time to think and create, and as a PhD student, it gave me more time to research.

Shortly after starting my assistantship in 2022, I was offered a spot in the grant program I had originally applied to as a full-time student. I was thrilled. That opportunity was a major blessing and opened doors that wouldn't have been available otherwise—it gave me one foot up. But just six months after receiving such exciting news, I was hit with devastating news that indefinitely shifted my state of being: my father passed away. The spiritual closeness we shared was intense. We had our lows, but we were more alike than I initially realized. In the months leading up to his passing, I had already started to feel different—something in me was changing spiritually. I was evolving, and my perspective had shifted significantly.

His transition triggered a massive spiritual awakening—some might call it psychosis. However it may be perceived, a state of physical absenteeism and spiritual heightenness persisted for six months. I continued my graduate work, but I couldn't interact with others properly. I isolated myself, endured multiple Baker Acts, and became increasingly sensitive to energies. Even as the mania simmered down, the overwhelming energies I encountered when around other people never fully subsided.

While I traveled through that experience in the second half of 2022, I spent the first half of 2023 disconnected from social media, trying to rebuild my life and piece together what I felt

I had destroyed with my children. In that process, I also questioned whether ending certain friendships had been worth it. Regardless, I didn't know how to face people again. I was in disbelief and deeply embarrassed by what felt like a public transgression—one that had been completely out of my control.

As graduation neared, I knew I wanted to move out of state. But in order to do that, I needed funds. So I decided to take on temporary work as a support facilitator with the school board. Yes, I already had a lot on my plate, but I believed temporary work wouldn't hurt me. I was wrong.

I had not been in a real workplace since 2021. Now that it was 2023, I knew returning to the K–12 environment would be challenging, but I figured a year wouldn't hurt. I made sure to sense the energy during the interview to see if it would be a good fit for me, given my past experiences. During the interview, the principal seemed very optimistic and positive. I interviewed for a middle school ESE support role because I knew I couldn't take on a full classroom with the amount of work I still needed to complete for my dissertation. I felt excited and thrilled by the idea of what I perceived would be an excellent environment based on the leadership.

The environment felt very light, the organizational structure was like a clan culture. The student population was diverse—Hispanic, Caribbean descent, African American, White, and Asian. The staff was diverse too. I worked alongside two other ESE support facilitators who had been in the field for a while—one Black and the other White. They immediately noticed that I didn't talk much. They were sweet, but I had learned my lessons years ago: never talk too much, because people were always gossiping. They assured me it was alright and that they were there if I needed anything.

I took on a caseload of approximately fifty sixth graders, so I needed to be well prepared. I organized folders, created notecards with accommodations, sent an email to all educators introducing my teaching style and availability, and messaged all parents as well. I was on a roll, and I was ready to be the best I could be for what I presume would be my last year working with the school board.

The only thing I disliked about the position was the duty schedule. They expected me to get up for every bell change, as if I didn't actually pull students out and teach. I had to do cafeteria duty too. But overall, the position was alright. The people I worked alongside were pleasant and helpful.

However, the peace I was maintaining didn't continue for much longer. Shortly after being hired, I discovered that the principal was leaving for a district-level position and another woman would be taking her place. Soon after the new principal arrived, I found that changes had to be made due to low student enrollment—which meant my position was being cut. I was given two options: become a reading teacher or transfer to another school that needed an ESE support facilitator.

Changes triggered overstimulation for me, and I was given a short window to make a drastic decision. I needed the funds to move later on, out-of-state, but I also needed to stay mentally stable to finish my dissertation and take care of my kids. I felt like the universe was against me, and I needed to understand why I had to make such a change. Why was the universe uprooting me like this?

I had already organized all student files, completed all introductions, and set myself up. And in less than two months, I had to pack up again and redo the whole process. I spoke with the principal and explained my mental health challenges. I told her I couldn't take on a full classroom because of overstimulation and the school schedule. She gave me options and told me there was one school—middle school—she thought would be a great fit for me and said I'd love it there.

I was distraught, but I tried to see the silver lining. And I did. When I looked up the school, I realized a former best friend—someone I'd severed ties with in 2022 after my dad's passing and during my spiritual awakening—worked there. I hadn't seen or spoken to her in over a year. Now, I was being placed in the same workplace. I thought maybe the powers that be were giving me an opportunity to explain how I felt during that time, to possibly gain closure or share the pain I had felt. Otherwise, I wouldn't have understood the reason for the sudden change that placed such strain on my mental health.

I made peace with the move. And although I was briefly at the current middle school, the ESE team threw me a going away party, which truly surprised me—I had never been celebrated like that at work before. That job, though brief, had the kind of clan culture that was of my liking. There weren't any severe issues I observed, and I saw myself thriving there in peace. But soon, I would be walking into a workplace culture I didn't understand and had no say in joining if I wanted to keep my job.

When I arrived at the new school, which was approximately an hour and a half away, I felt a very heavy energy in the atmosphere. The principal at my former school had misread me and directed me in the wrong direction. I assumed she thought this environment would be good for me simply because it was a predominantly Black school. However, she had made assumptions based on my physical traits and overt culture, completely unaware of my covert culture.

I preferred to be surrounded by open-minded, lighthearted, introspective, and grounded individuals. While I valued working with culturally diverse people, it didn't mean I wanted to be in a space filled with hostility and constant gossip. Immediately, my spirit was shaken. I knew then that this culture, despite the principal's claims of being a "family," was most definitely a Hostile Hierarchical Culture. The principal displayed narcissistic traits, and it was clear that people were afraid to speak their minds.

Right away, I didn't have access to everything I needed, but yet the principal called the ESE support team to her office, which consisted of me and another Caribbean Muslim woman. She explained that we had to complete certain IEPs in order to secure funding. She requested that I help with IEPs for students I hadn't even met yet. I ended up with a caseload of nearly seven students. I had to organize everything in the way I had at my former school—contacting parents and managing files—and within the timeframe the principal demanded, I uncomfortably completed eight IEPs even though I wasn't the file holder.

Right around this time, I saw my best friend—the same friend I had suddenly withdrawn from without notice. The moment

I saw her, I felt her intense energy. She was doing her best to act like she didn't care, but I could tell she was hurt. After completing those IEPs, I decided I needed to approach her—not necessarily to reconcile, but to reach a certain level of understanding. I asked if I could speak with her. I believe I tapped her shoulder, and she moved as if she didn't want to be touched by me. Still, she walked me back to her office. I opened up to her about what I had gone through and how I felt in situations where the love I gave wasn't reciprocated by her. She sat with her arms crossed, her energy rejecting me before even trying to understand. I could tell she was operating from a place of hurt—her ego. Everything I mentioned, she had a defense for or claimed not to recall, which hurt even more. But I had to let her know that I wasn't the same person anymore, and that I love more deeply now, and I understand that not everyone can reciprocate the kind of unconditional love I have. The conversation didn't go as I hoped, but I suppose I was grateful that I at least tried. I needed some kind of closure.

Meanwhile, I was busy trying to meet expectations quickly so I could avoid interacting with the administration, especially the principal. She gave off strong narcissistic energy. In meetings, she talked at length about her accolades. When I suggested a method to help with the school's behavioral issues, she never replied to my email. Yet, I later noticed she used part of my suggestion—handing out tickets to students for a system they had in place but had barely used. It felt like a backhanded acknowledgment, with no collaboration or credit.

She also introduced a team-building game during a planning day and claimed she had thought of it herself. But I had played that same game at my previous school, likely passed down through a principal's meeting. It seemed like she wanted to take credit for everything. She often talked at the staff instead of collaborating with us. When I visited classrooms, staff would rant and complain about their experiences with her.

A co-worker from my former school, an Asian woman who had joined as a coach, also commented on the "heavy" energy at the school. It was dark. It triggered flashbacks to my first teaching job as a first grade teacher. I always believed that employees are only as good as their leader. A leader with toxic energy, obsessed with showing everyone "who's boss," can bring down an entire organization.

Shortly after starting at the school, I began to feel overwhelmed and spiritually captivated. Half the staff were deeply spiritual, while the other half were egotistical. I tried to focus on my students and on aligning with my spiritual purpose, but it was difficult in a space where many people didn't understand the weight of what happens in the unseen.

One day, a custodian stopped me and told me I was going through a lot, but that I was heavily protected. He read me on the spot. We later had deeper conversations where he shared his spiritual gifts with me. There was a woman from Barbados who called me "queen" and told me she saw me, meaning that she saw my aura, my light. An older Black woman hugged me and called me her daughter, saying I was beautiful from within. I also had meaningful conversations with a Haitian woman who told me I was different and that I wasn't meant to be understood.

These conversations became increasingly spiritual, and within a couple of months, I found myself withdrawing. One teacher came to me and asked, "If we are gods, what does that mean?" Then she went on to explain her perspective. I felt myself slipping into the spiritual realm, trying hard to avoid administration so they wouldn't notice or start questioning me.

But that avoidance didn't last. I started using my social media more to engage in spiritually deep discussions. Over time, the energy at work became even more intense. Coupled with the toxic environment and the long commute, I began displaying manic traits. By November, people were talking about me more. I noticed more watchful eyes, more people being nosy without asking questions directly.

I tried to keep a low profile, but I attracted attention when I had used my social media as an outlet to voice some of my more unfiltered, deranged thoughts. While attending a required training, police officers pulled me out to question my post. They said someone had reported it and asked if I was going to harm myself or anyone else; I suppose it was a welfare check. Although I was not a 100 percent myself, I had been aware of the right and wrong things to say, but I did go on a little rant about society. The issue wasn't me, but this cruel society.

After that meeting, I took down the post and made everything private. I had not been aware that people were watching my social media profile, but apparently, there were people at that school keeping a very close eye on me. Toward the end of school, before winter break, the mania had increased and euphoria was at an all-time high. Random people approached me with insightful conversations. I had another heartfelt conversation with my ex-best friend about the new insight I had received. I felt liberated, but being liberated in a restricted place had its consequences.

Each day nearing the end of the semester became increasingly intense, and I was becoming even more disconnected from the physical realm. However, I was still able to complete all work required of me: I hosted IEP meetings, I assisted educators and students alike, and I clearly communicated with parents. Then a couple of days before the last day of school, I felt the intensity of putting myself at risk of being involuntarily institutionalized in a psychiatric ward. So I asked the other ESE support facilitator to let them know that I had to go. I didn't want anyone to see me. I disappeared from the scene to avoid being judged by people who had no idea what was going on or how to handle me.

Mania was in full effect. I had begun to recognize signs in everything and started making connections that others didn't understand.

During the winter break, I ended up being Baker Acted (involuntarily committed) for a few days, but I was able to get out within a couple of days. Later, during the new year, I attended a conference and presented while battling full-fledged mania. My sister was there with me, and I was grateful for that, but the travel and being there was intense because I would not stop talking. Still, I managed to present without seeming off.

However, once I returned to work, it was a different situation. I was running late for work and messaged the school letting them know I had overslept, which was a good thing because I needed to get some sleep. When I reached work, I was immediately called to the office. At that time, I was unaware that my sister had reached out to my principal about me being unwell before winter break—it was her attempt to protect my job because I did walk off, but I had also asked the other support facilitator to let them know. My sister did not tell them what was going on; she just said I was not well.

Unaware the principal had this information, I walked into her office with the two other APs, and immediately I felt I was being bombarded. When a supervisor was dealing with anyone battling mania, the best thing to do was give them space: do not argue with them, even if you did not agree with them, just listen without judgment, ask how you could help, and more importantly, do not take anything they said or did personally. This principal did everything but that. She also was the one who had reported my social media, which I later found out.

The first thing she said when I walked into the office was a reminder of what time I was supposed to report to work as if I didn't know. I had never been late before, but she decided it was necessary to remind me, which showed a lack of empathy for my situation. She was forcing herself on me without an attempt to genuinely support me. Instantly, I found myself boiling inside because her approach was ingenuine. She then recommended an ESS (Employee Self-Service) service that would provide me with options for therapy. I ended up ranting, letting her know that I had been through this before and therapy was not even helpful when someone was manic because you were bouncing off the walls and could not possibly sit still to listen.

I exploded and walked away. As soon as I walked away, I went to my room to put in a hardship transfer request because I knew I could not stand to work there any longer. I lived far away, so I knew it would be approved. Once I turned in the transfer request, I was met with a write-up for insubordination or something of the sort the next day, and immediately I knew she was retaliating because I had requested a transfer.

I stormed into her office and told her that she was going to get what she deserved. I lost full control and people saw. My ex-best friend tried to calm me down, and later other people tried to talk to me. I viewed her as an egotistical demon; she might have been worse than the principal from the first school I had ever worked. Later that day, I was told to pack my stuff and leave, as I was later placed on paid leave pending a psych evaluation.

In hindsight, it was a blessing in disguise because I had to complete my dissertation without the stress—I was free. However, she had pushed me out of a school that needed my assistance due to her need for control, and when a narcissistic person was given truth they could not take, they became filled with anger.

Furthermore, pushing someone who was battling with mania out of their routine could cause the mania to progress. I had been pushed out of my normal routine, which allowed me to run free in nature and do whatever suited me. Oddly enough, I kept up with my requirements for my dissertation, but I could not keep up with parenting and the hygiene of my kids and, at times, myself. Everything escalated, and during this time, I received a phone call from the school board for an appointment to meet with a psychiatrist. But I did not recall the phone call, and the worst thing to do was to remind someone battling mania via phone call because it was not possible that they would—or could—retain information. It should have been in writing.

I was not taking care of my daily duties, and my mail was overflowing; some was even sent back to the post office—the mail that apparently had the information about a scheduled appointment I did not attend. Later on, I received an email letting me know that the school board had tried to reach me, but now I was going to due process because I had not attended the appointment.

At that moment, it was March and the mania had started to die down. I was leaving the school board regardless, but I refused to be pushed out; I was going to leave on my own terms. My mom had connected me with someone from the teacher union. Although I had not been part of the union—because I did not see the point since I knew I was just going to complete one year and leave—they were trying to push me out and leave me in bad standing. The rep from the teacher union was very familiar with the principal, and she said that I should've joined the union as soon as I transferred to that school. She said she had received many complaints about the principal. She said I should have known better—pretty much expressing that it was obvious the woman was an evil-acting person.

And although I knew I would not return, I did not want to be in bad standing. So, before everything went down the drain, I gathered all the necessary documents to gain my certification in two other states, Oklahoma and Georgia, just in case I did not get a higher ed position right away.

Also, to fight the case, I submitted a request to the disability department to file a complaint for discrimination due to disability. During this time, many people were interviewed, and in the end, I did not have sufficient information as proof of discrimination, but the lady resonated with me and commended me for my situation. Ultimately, my filing for discrimination triggered the office that worked on fit-for-duty assessments to reopen my case and allow me to continue on paid leave as I continued my psych evaluation, which took longer than anticipated.

The school board had not handled my situation appropriately, and during my case, I was made aware of more than I had expected or anticipated. People at that school did not have a strong sense of unity and did not care to speak truth to that principal. The ESE support facilitator, who I had asked to sit in the meeting with me, explained that she felt it was best she did not—I guess due to her job. Oddly, a year later, she contacted me asking for help because she was having issues with that same principal. She had refused to do what the principal was asking of her because it was too much and above her pay grade. I assisted my former co-worker, but I did not overextend; she, too, ended up leaving the school.

This situation just went to show how much courage people lacked in a hostile, hierarchical culture. And when you found yourself against the tide of injustices, you almost always found yourself standing alone. But karma had a way of showing people themselves.

Conclusion

In the closing chapter, I reflect on what I've learned throughout my journey, the choices I would change, and how I now manage my mental health and identity in a healthier way.

Closing my chapter of working with the sixth largest school district in the nation as a teacher was bittersweet. Had the atmosphere I worked in been more welcoming, I could have remained an educator while simultaneously finishing school. I realized that I could not handle large settings for prolonged periods. After leaving Florida, I moved across the country to work in one of the smallest school districts in Oklahoma. Coming from a hostile environment into a more welcoming, friendlier one, I discovered that I could endure an entire school year without becoming overwhelmingly wired and agitated. I thrived in Clan Organizational Cultures where everyone worked together to achieve a common goal.

The culture I moved into in Oklahoma was also predominantly White. Initially, I was concerned because I had never worked in a predominantly White space and did not want others to feel uncomfortable or feel like they had to monitor what they said around me. I noticed that some were uneasy at first, trying to engage with the only Black woman in the building. However, I used my ability to read people and initiated light conversation, which I believe made others more comfortable. Although I did not socialize with everyone, I noticed that within the White population in this rural area, people seemed to hold less hostility toward one another—there was a stronger sense of community. It was a breath of fresh air. Working in a small school district taught me that I could manage environments with several people as long as those people carried light energy.

Throughout my journey in K–12 public school systems, I learned not to take things personally. While it was difficult to ignore negative energies, I came to understand that everyone has their own battles and many walk around projecting. The best way I found to protect myself was to keep things light, keep conversations short, and let people know that I welcome transparency and to correct me if I offend. In hindsight, I would have handled certain situations more proactively and less reactively.

My first position taught me the dynamics of public education, and although I wouldn't change anything, those early moments made me stronger and more equipped to handle unexpected challenges, like sudden changes in schedules. My second position taught me to leave while things were still good. I enjoyed that job and stayed for four consecutive years, but I knew when my time was up. That awareness—knowing when a situation has run its course—is critical in any job.

As a working-class citizen, I also learned that when you know a lot and work hard, people may take advantage of you. It's important to recognize your limits and advocate for yourself accordingly. One change I would have made earlier was to open up less. At my last job in the small district, I remained more guarded. I did eventually share my diagnosis, but not until the last month of school. Surprisingly, I felt fine doing so and noticed that it encouraged others to share personal stories of their own. That moment revealed something important to me: the Black community has so much growing to do. We must evolve to understand that mental health is a topic we can—and should—talk about. We must dismantle the stigma so we can support each other better.

I escaped South Florida to get away from "my" community due to the judgment and the gossip. Ironically, I ran to a community historically known for being the dominant culture and felt more comfortable than I ever had within my own. That revelation hurt. Realizing that the same people you are quick to support are often the ones who push you away when you display even the smallest difference from their facade was painful.

I also discovered that I was more triggered by overall injustices than by those directly against me. It hurt to see others unable to defend themselves or too fearful of losing their jobs to speak up. I learned not to sweat the small stuff, but I also found my voice and spoke up when I felt an organization was doing a disservice to its staff.

This journey revealed many of my weaknesses but also highlighted my strengths. I never allowed anything to deter me from my main goal. I navigated the K–12 system for seven years, took a necessary two-year leave to focus on school, and ultimately reached my goal of moving into higher education as an assistant professor.

The trials and tribulations I endured as an unorthodox Black woman with a mental health diagnosis were insurmountable at times—but I made it through. My mental strength grew tremendously. I developed a sharper awareness of when an "episode" was approaching and learned to reduce my interactions during those periods. I also came to accept that even when people seem to understand, they often don't. I now realize my steps are guided, and as I navigate different systems, I must be hyperaware of what I share because not everyone will receive it with understanding.

My covert culture does not align with most Black Americans, nor with Muslims, nor entirely with people with disabilities. I do not see myself as having a disability but rather a gift—one that may make me different but has led me to places many others are afraid to go. I respect the Black community for its spirited creativity, the energy it brings to any space, and the raw authenticity you feel when you're among it. But my identity today is the same as it was at the beginning of my journey—disconnected from the cultures I was born into and raised in.

My identity is rooted in my innate ability to see the beauty in all living things, to resonate with others, to empathize, and to love unconditionally. Though many may not understand me—or may think I am too eccentric for the workplace—I have learned that most people operate from ego while I remain focused on aligning with my higher self. Whether in a hostile, hierarchical, or clan-like environment, I know I will succeed. With every transition came wisdom, and I am sure to spark the flame in others wherever I go.

In reflecting on this journey, I see not only the lessons learned but the ways in which I've evolved—emotionally, mentally, and spiritually. I would make different choices now, but I understand that every step brought clarity. Most importantly, I've learned how to manage my mental health and identity on my own terms, with compassion, self-awareness, and resilience.

Discussion questions

After reading this book, I invite you to reflect on the following questions and discuss them within your current organizational culture or with classmates. Together, we can explore how to better support one another and help dismantle the stigma surrounding mental illness.

- How does workplace culture impact mental health and professional growth, especially for individuals from marginalized backgrounds?
- In what ways can we learn to recognize when it's time to leave a job or environment that no longer serves us?
- How can conversations about mental health be normalized within communities that have historically stigmatized it?
- What role does identity play in how we navigate professional spaces, and how can we honor our individuality while adapting to different environments?
- Have you ever felt more accepted or understood in a space outside your own community? What did that experience teach you about belonging and connection?

Recommended further readings

- **Bell Hooks**, *Sisters of the Yam: Black Women and Self-Recovery*. An essential text addressing healing, mental wellness, and self-love among Black women.
- **Patricia Hill Collins**, *Black Feminist Thought*. A foundational academic work on intersectionality, identity, and the lived experience of Black women.
- **Tunsill, Buruuj**, *Memoirs of a Single Mother*. This personal narrative offers a powerful account of Black womanhood, single motherhood, and the pursuit of stability while managing mental health challenges. Through deeply reflective storytelling, this book explores the intersection of identity, resilience, and the emotional labor of navigating societal expectations. It complements the proposed work by offering further insight into lived experiences often overlooked in mainstream mental health and academic discourse.

Index

www.ingramcontent.com/pod-product-compliance
Lightning Source LLC
Chambersburg PA
CBHW070349270326
41926CB00017B/4058